Strategic READING 1
Building Effective Reading Skills

Teacher's Manual

CAMBRIDGE
UNIVERSITY PRESS

Lynn Bonesteel

PUBLISHED BY THE PRESS SYNDICATE OF THE UNIVERSITY OF CAMBRIDGE
The Pitt Building, Trumpington Street, Cambridge, United Kingdom

CAMBRIDGE UNIVERSITY PRESS
The Edinburgh Building, Cambridge CB2 2RU, UK
40 West 20th Street, New York, NY 10011–4211, USA
10 Stamford Road, Oakleigh, VIC 3166, Australia
Ruiz de Alarcón 13, 28014 Madrid, Spain
Dock House, The Waterfront, Cape Town 8001, South Africa

http://www.cambridge.org

First published 2003

Printed in the United States of America

Typeface Adobe Caslon (Adobe®) System QuarkXPress® [AH]

A catalog record for this book is available from the British Library
Library of Congress Cataloging in Publication data available

ISBN 0 521 555809   Student's Book 1
ISBN 0 521 555779   Teacher's Manual 1
ISBN 0 521 555795   Student's Book 2
ISBN 0 521 555760   Teacher's Manual 2

Illustrations:
Art direction, book design, and layout services: Adventure House, NYC

Contents

Introduction   v

Model lesson plan   ix

Teaching suggestions   1

UNIT 1   **Music**   1

UNIT 2   **Money**   7

UNIT 3   **Work**   12

UNIT 4   **Sports**   17

UNIT 5   **Weather**   23

UNIT 6   **Clothes**   28

UNIT 7   **Culture**   33

UNIT 8   **Outer space**   37

UNIT 9   **Animals**   42

UNIT 10   **Travel**   47

UNIT 11   **The Internet**   51

UNIT 12   **Friends**   56

U N I T 1 3	Gifts	60
U N I T 1 4	Emotions	64
U N I T 1 5	Food	70
U N I T 1 6	Sleep & dreams	76
	Unit quizzes	81
	Unit quiz answers	97

Introduction

Strategic Reading: Building Effective Reading Skills is a three-level series for young-adult and adult learners of English. As its title suggests, it is designed to develop useful reading, vocabulary-building, and critical thinking skills. Each level features adapted texts from a variety of authentic sources, including newspapers, magazines, books, and websites. The series encourages students to examine important topics in their lives as they build essential reading skills.

The first level in the series, *Strategic Reading 1*, is aimed at low-intermediate to intermediate students. It contains 16 units divided into three readings on popular themes such as music, travel, friendship, and outer space.

Every unit begins by introducing new vocabulary and asking questions related to the theme. Each reading ranges in length from 350 to 450 words and is accompanied by a full page of activities. Pre-reading activities interest students in the lesson topic, while reading exercises develop crucial skills and provide opportunities for discussion and writing. The wrap-up at the end of each unit recycles and expands key vocabulary into additional exercises and puzzles. Engaging extension activities serve as a valuable link to the world outside the classroom.

Each unit is designed to take five to six hours of class time, if all the activities are completed and the readings are assigned as class work. The units (and the readings within units) can either be taught in the order they appear or out of sequence. The readings and exercises, however, increase in difficulty throughout the book. The reading skills developed in these exercises are listed and indexed in the Scope and sequence on pages vi-ix of the Student's Book.

Student's Book organization
Preview

Every unit begins with a brief summary of each reading in the unit. These summaries are followed by questions for writing or discussion. The questions stimulate students' interest in the readings and allow them to share their knowledge about the topic. In addition, vocabulary from the readings appears on the preview page. As students discuss the preview questions, they should be encouraged to ask about unfamiliar vocabulary.

A separate vocabulary exercise familiarizes students with vocabulary related to the unit theme. Pre-teaching this vocabulary gives students a chance to relate the words to their lives and also helps them feel more comfortable as they begin to read. The new vocabulary words appear several times throughout the unit, providing students with more opportunities to learn their meanings and uses.

Before you read

Before each reading, students complete one of four types of pre-reading exercises: *Predicting, Relating to the topic, Thinking about personal experience,* or *Using previous knowledge.* These exercises prepare students to read and help them connect the topic of the reading to their own lives. Students mark statements that are true about themselves, identify information they expect to read, and write down what they expect to learn.

Reading

One *Scanning* or *Skimming* exercise accompanies every reading. Students learn to either scan or skim a text to look for specific information before reading the whole text. Other activities in this section ask students to confirm predictions from the "Before you read" section, compare their experiences with the author's experiences or identify the author's purpose, opinion, tone, or intended audience.

After you read

The varied exercises in this section provide practice in all aspects of a skill and accommodate different learning and teaching styles. Skills and activities in this section focus on:

- **Main ideas** Students choose the main idea of a reading or a paragraph or identify an author's opinion or point of view.

- **Details** Students show their understanding of details or distinguish between a main idea and a detail.

- **Guessing vocabulary from context** Students use contextual clues, recognize similarity in meaning between words, or recognize different forms of word families.

- **Text organization** Students show understanding of reference words or add sentences to a paragraph.

- **Restatement and inference** Students make inferences based on the text or distinguish between a restatement and an inference.

The final exercise, *Relating reading to personal experience*, asks three open-ended questions that are closely connected to the topic of the reading. It gives students an opportunity to share their thoughts, opinions, and experiences in writing or in discussions. It is also a chance to review and use vocabulary introduced in the unit.

Wrap-up

Every unit ends with a one-page wrap-up. In these exercises, students use vocabulary from the unit. Although some of this vocabulary appears in the readings, new terms may be introduced here.

The final exercise provides an opportunity for students to use the vocabulary they have learned in a meaningful context. Students work on a project, prepare a presentation, or participate in a discussion related to the unit theme. These activities involve designing and conducting surveys, researching and giving presentations, or interviewing classmates or native speakers of English.

Reading tips

Every unit features a reading tip designed to provide students with a useful language point illustrated in the reading. These tips correspond to the reading skills that students practice after reading.

Vocabulary

Students are sometimes instructed to find out the meaning of words or phrases. There are several ways that you can suggest students do this:

- Work together to help each other with unfamiliar vocabulary.

- Ask you (or a native speaker) to explain unfamiliar words.

- Look up the meanings of unfamiliar words in an English dictionary, such as the *Cambridge Dictionary of American English*.

- Use a bilingual dictionary or pocket translator to look up words that are hard to explain (for example, the names of animals or sports). In general, however, the use of bilingual dictionaries is not recommended.

Teacher's Manual organization

A Teacher's Manual is available for each level of *Strategic Reading*. Each Teacher's Manual contains:

- a model lesson plan,
- specific teaching suggestions for each unit in the Student's Book, including additional vocabulary definitions, cultural notes, and answers to exercises in the Student's Book,
- photocopiable unit quizzes, and
- answers to unit quizzes.

Teaching suggestions

Teaching suggestions for each unit offer specific ideas on how to present the material and additional vocabulary. Only vocabulary items that are not defined or represented pictorially in the Student's Book have been included. These items are defined as they are used in the reading. In addition, variations and optional activities have been provided to further expand upon reading topics, vocabulary, and exercises. Answers to the exercises in the Student's Book and some explanations have also been provided.

Unit quizzes

Photocopiable quizzes for each unit can be found at the back of this Teacher's Manual. Each quiz contains a 150- to 175-word reading related to the unit theme and a half-page of reading skills exercises. The quizzes measure general reading comprehension and ability to use basic reading strategies. Every quiz includes a *Guessing meaning from context* vocabulary exercise. Although individual vocabulary items are not tested separately, some of the unit vocabulary appears in each quiz reading. Suggested scores are included in the direction lines of all exercises. An answer key for all the quizzes can also be found at the back of the book.

Model lesson plan

Each unit of *Strategic Reading 1* can be divided into five lessons — one preview lesson, three lessons based on readings, and one wrap-up lesson. The entire unit should take approximately five to six hours to complete.

This lesson plan can serve as a generic outline to guide you through a lesson. It can be used with any unit of the Student's Book. For specific ideas on how the material can be presented or further expanded, refer to the Teaching suggestions for each unit.

Preview

The summaries, questions, and vocabulary on the preview page are intended to get the students interested in the readings and give them an opportunity to share their knowledge about reading topics.

Theme *(approximately 20-30 minutes)*

1. Give students a few minutes to read the preview questions. As students read, circulate and answer questions.

2. When students have read the questions, have them form pairs to discuss their answers. Tell them they will report at least one of their partner's answers to the class.

3. After 15–20 minutes, ask several students to share something their partners told them.

> *Variations*:
> - Assign step 1 as homework.
> - Assign step 2 as a small group discussion. Have each group report on something interesting from their discussion.
> - Ask students to answer the unit preview questions in writing, either at home or in class. Have them read their partner's responses in class and compare them to their own responses.

Vocabulary *(approximately 15-20 minutes)*

1. Tell students they will be learning new vocabulary that they need for the readings in the unit.

2. Choose a word from the vocabulary exercise. Write it on the board, and ask questions related to the word and the unit theme.

3. Have students complete the vocabulary exercise in pairs. Encourage them to use examples when they explain the meanings of words. Allow the use of dictionaries only if neither student knows the word.

4. After a few minutes, reassemble the class and help students with any words they still don't know.

> **Variation:**
> • Have students complete the vocabulary exercise as homework and discuss any unknown words in class.

Reading 1

Before you read *(approximately 10-15 minutes)*

This section prepares students to read and helps them connect the topic of the reading to their own lives.

1. Explain the meanings of any unfamiliar words in the title of the reading.

2. Tell students to work alone on the *Thinking about personal experience* exercise. If necessary, they can refer to the vocabulary exercise on the Preview page. Help them with any unfamiliar vocabulary.

3. After a few minutes, elicit their responses. Write the results on the board.

> **Variation:**
> • Assign step 2 as pair or group work.

Reading *(approximately 15-20 minutes)*

This section provides students with valuable practice in reading for general or specific information. Before beginning, make sure students understand the difference between reading a text and skimming or scanning it. Explain that *skimming* is a quick reading for general ideas. You do not read carefully; instead, you look at the title, subtitles, charts, pictures, and graphs to find out about the text. *Scanning* is also a quick reading, but here you look for information to answer a specific question, such as a number, name, word, or phrase.

1. Have students complete the *Skimming* or *Scanning* exercise. Tell students to raise their hands when they think they have the correct answers. After a minute or two, ask the students who raised their hands first and check the answers.

2. Give the class about five to seven minutes to read the entire article. Students who finish early should begin to read the article again. Slower readers should push themselves to finish the passage in the given time. Do not allow students to use dictionaries during the first reading. Instead, suggest that students focus on main ideas and ignore or guess unfamiliar vocabulary. Explain that they will have an opportunity later to learn the unfamiliar words later.

After you read *(approximately 40-50 minutes)*

The purpose of these activities is to develop specific reading skills.

1. Tell students to work individually on the first exercise. Answer the first item together to make sure students understand the exercise. After a few minutes, have them compare their answers with a partner and discuss any differences. As they work, circulate and check their answers.

2. Have students complete the second exercise in pairs. Explain the purpose of the exercise (indicated in the Teaching suggestions), and answer the first item together.

3. When students finish, go over the exercise. Ask individual students to explain their answers.

4. Have students discuss the questions in *Relating reading to personal experience* in pairs. After about ten minutes, ask several students to share one of their answers.

Follow the plan outlined above for the second and third readings in each unit. Try to vary the use of individual, pair, small group, and whole-class activities. You may choose to follow the same basic steps, but use some of the suggested variations to keep the lessons lively. To practice expressing their ideas in writing, students should write their answers to at least one of the *Predicting* and one of the *Relating reading to personal experience* exercises in each unit. Encourage students to use new vocabulary from the unit when they write. When possible, collect their work and return it to them with your comments.

Wrap-up *(approximately 60 minutes)*

The purpose of this page is to provide an opportunity for students to review and apply new vocabulary in a meaningful context.

1. Have students work alone on the Vocabulary expansion exercise(s). Use one item as an example to make sure that students understand the task. When students are finished, have them check their answers in pairs.

2. Follow the instructions for the final activity on the Wrap-up page. Although these activities usually involve student interaction, others are appropriate for individual or pair work.

3. Tell students that there will be a quiz on the unit based on their comprehension and reading skills, not on specific vocabulary. Point out that the reading passage in the quiz will contain some vocabulary from the unit.

> *Variations:*
> - Use the Vocabulary expansion exercise(s) as a competition. Divide the class into teams of three or four students each. Set a time limit to complete the activity. The team that finishes the activity first is the winner.
> - The Vocabulary expansion exercise(s) can also be assigned as homework.
> - After the students complete all the exercises on the Wrap-up page, a variety of games and activities can be used to review the unit vocabulary.

Additional vocabulary

brilliant: extremely intelligent or highly skilled

express: show a feeling or idea

jazz: a type of music of African-American origin with a strong rhythm

mood: the way you feel at a particular time

note: a single sound in music or a written symbol that represents this sound

Additional activity

After students complete the vocabulary exercise, review the meanings of some of the target words. Write a column on the board with examples of a particular word, but leave the heading for each column blank. For example, you could write the following on the board, and have the students fill in the missing category names.

1. _____	2. _____	3. _____
Mozart	tango	E flat
Beethoven	salsa	C sharp
Handel	mambo	G natural

Answers: 1. classical composers, 2. Latin music, 3. musical notes

Music & moods

This reading explains the effect of music on people's emotions.

Additional vocabulary

accented: with special emphasis given to a syllable in a word, word in a sentence, or musical note

beat: defeat; a rhythmic sound

cheer up: feel happier

music therapy: the use of music to treat someone who suffers from a mental or physical problem

percussion: musical instruments, such as drums, that are played by being hit with an object or with the hand

pick up: start doing at a faster rate

continued on next page

put on: play on a sound system, such as a CD player
rush: a sudden strong emotion or physical feeling
take advantage of: use an opportunity to achieve results
tempo: the speed at which a piece of music is played
tune: a series of musical notes; a melody or song

Guessing meaning from context

Students are often uncomfortable reading without a dictionary. It's important to spend time developing this skill in the beginning of the term. Below are step-by-step instructions on how to introduce this skill:

1. Tell students that they are going to focus on understanding unfamiliar vocabulary in the text without using a dictionary. Direct their attention to exercise B on page 3, using *beat a bad mood* as an example.

2. Have students read paragraph 1 again, paying special attention to the target expression. Ask students to circle the words in the paragraph that led them to the correct answer. Call on individual students to answer. Then discuss how the context helped them guess the meaning as a class.

3. Have students work alone on the remaining six items in the exercise. Make sure they circle the words or phrases in the text that help them figure out the answer. After 10–15 minutes, tell them to compare their answers with their partner. If they have different answers, they should go back to the text and show each other the words they circled. If they still cannot agree on an answer, they should ask you or another classmate. As students work, circulate to help.

4. When students have finished, go over the answers as a class. Have them go back to the text to indicate the words they circled. Point out any contextual clues they missed.

STRATEGY: Encourage students to circle the words in the paragraph that lead them to the correct answer.

ANSWERS
Reading
1, 2, 3, 4, 5
After you read
A
a. 4   b. 2   c. 1   d. 3
B
1. stops   5. do not pay attention
2. energetic   6. peaceful and calm
3. more   7. slow love song
4. difficult

Cultural notes

Frank Sinatra Born in 1915 in Hoboken, New Jersey, Frank Sinatra became one of the most famous popular singers of his generation, and perhaps of all time. Many people consider him to be the greatest interpreter of popular songs the world has known. He was especially well-known for the way he interpreted songs about love and romance.

Aretha Franklin Aretha Franklin was born in 1942. She started out as a gospel[1] singer in Detroit, Michigan, and became famous in the 1960s and 70s for her unique blend of gospel, blues, pop, and rock. Known as "Lady Soul," she is one of the most admired soul[2] artists of all time. She is best known for her energetic, passionate, and intense songs, including the extremely popular song "Respect."

1 Gospel music is a style of Christian religious music originally developed and performed by African Americans.

2 Soul music is a type of popular music with a strong beat and rhythm that developed from gospel music.

READING 2 Louis Armstrong

Pages 4-5

This reading presents a biography of the world-famous jazz musician.

Additional vocabulary

all over: completely
boys' home: a place where young boys who have committed a crime are sent to live
celebrated: famous for a special quality or ability
equal: a person who is as important as someone else
genius: a person with very great natural ability or skill
humanity: understanding and kindness toward other people
minor: not very important
offense: a crime
tale: a story or report, especially one that is difficult to believe
teens: the teenage years
tough: violent or containing violence
vocal: relating to or produced by the voice

Reading skill

Understanding details

When students complete true or false exercises, ask them to correct the false statements to make them true. This way, you can make sure that they understand the specific question, and are not simply guessing the answer.

Additional activity

Bringing in objects related to the readings will make the lessons livelier. Play one recording of Armstrong singing, and another of him playing the trumpet. Then, have students who are familiar with his music tell the others what they know about him.

READING 3   The biology of music

Pages 6-7

This reading explores the connection between music and the human brain.

Additional vocabulary

evidence: anything that helps to prove something
fitness: suitability for something
independently: without influence or control by another person, event, or thing
show off: do something to attract attention to yourself
stroke: a sudden change in the blood supply to a part of the brain, which can result in a loss of mental or physical abilities, or death

Reading skill

Distinguishing main and supporting ideas

Ask students to give their answers to exercise B. If students think a statement is an example, ask them to find the general statement that the example supports. If students think a statement is general, ask them to find an example in the text that supports the general statement.

ANSWERS

Reading

1, 2, 5

After you read

A

4. serious

B

1. general statement (The example is in par. 4: For example, Vissarion . . .)
2. specific example (The general statement is item 1.)
3. general statement (The examples are in par. 5: Singing in tune, or playing a musical instrument . . . control. Remembering the notes . . . memory. Getting those notes right . . . condition.)
4. specific example (The general statement is item 3.)

WRAP-UP
Page 8

Additional vocabulary

blues: a type of music originating among African-American musicians in the southern United States in which the singer often sings about his or her difficult life and bad luck in love

classical: a form of music developed from a European tradition

rap: a type of popular music of African-American origin that features rhythmic speaking set to a strong beat

rock: a type of popular music with a strong beat, which is usually played with electric guitars and drums

POSSIBLE ANSWERS

A

People who make music: band, choir, composer, drummer, guitarist, musician, orchestra, singer, songwriter, trumpeter; *added words*: chorus, conductor, vocalist

Kinds of music: blues, classical, jazz, Latin, rap, rock; *added words*: folk, soul, gospel, hip-hop, pop

Musical instruments: cello, clarinet, cymbals, drums, flute, guitar, oboe, tambourine, trumpet, violin; *added words*: bass, synthesizer, harmonica

Musical terms: beat, note, tempo, tune; *added words*: a cappella, key signature, measure

continued on next page

B

1. beat, cello, clarinet, classical, composer, cymbals, flute, musician, note, oboe, tempo, trumpet, trumpeter, tune, violin; *added word*: conductor
2. beat, Latin, musician, note, singer, songwriter, tempo, tune; *added word*: pop
3. beat, drummer, drums, guitar, guitarist, musician, note, rock, singer, songwriter, tempo, tune; *added word*: heavy metal

Additional activity

Games are an excellent way to have students review the unit vocabulary. Here is one suggestion:

1. Before class, prepare a set of 20 vocabulary cards with one word or expression from the unit written on each card. Choose words or expressions that are easy to draw.

2. Divide the class into teams of three or four students each. Explain that you will show one person on each team the same word or expression. Then, they will have to draw a picture to get their teammates to guess the word. Tell them that the "artists" may not say or write any words.

3. The first team to guess the word gets a point. Then, another artist is assigned for each group.

PREVIEW
Page 9

Additional activity

Ask students to bring in paper money or coins from their country, as well as money from any other countries they have visited. Bring in some American, Canadian, British, or Australian currency. Pass the money around, and have the students discuss the meanings of any symbols and/or pictures. Ask students to research symbols or pictures that no one is able to explain.

READING 1 Dangers in shopping

Pages 10-11

This reading explains how shopping is an addiction for some people.

Additional vocabulary

deny: say something is not true
fully: completely
harmless: not able or likely to cause injury or damage
mastery: complete control
purchases: the things that you have bought
self-defeating: done in a way that keeps you from succeeding
urge: a strong desire or need

Reading skill

Understanding details

Explain to students that they shouldn't read the whole text again when they answer detail questions. Instead, suggest that they write the question number next to the place in the text where the answer is located. That way, they can refer back to the text more easily when explaining their answers.

STRATEGY: Encourage students to scan the text to find and underline the places in the text where they find the information.

ANSWERS
Reading
If students answered *yes* or *sometimes* to numbers 1, 2, 3, or 4, they might have a shopping problem.

After you read
A

1. e	2. d	3. a	4. f	5. b	6. c

continued on next page

B

1. b (par. 2: Most people think of shopping as something we do when we need to buy things . . .)
2. a (par. 3: People get into the dangerous habit of spending money to try to feel good.)
3. b (par. 5: . . . or strongly deny them. Compulsive spenders prefer to avoid the issues that force them to shop . . .)
4. a (par. 6: Some spontaneous spending is natural . . .)

READING 2 *Pages 12-13* # How to be a millionaire

This reading looks at the ways ordinary people become millionaires.

Additional vocabulary

eat away at: use so that little or nothing is left
far more: a lot more
generation: the usual period of time from a person's birth to the birth of his or her children
likely: probable
modest: not large in size or amount
optometrist: a person trained to test eyesight and prescribe glasses or contact lenses
pickup truck: a vehicle with an open part at the back to carry things
roofing contractors: workers who build and fix roofs
scrap-metal dealers: people who sell used metal so that it can be used again
stock: a part of the ownership of a company that people buy as an investment
stockbroker: a person or company that buys and sells stocks for other people
survey: collect information by asking many people the same questions, usually to find out how they live or their opinions about different things
tend to: be likely to

Reading skill

Understanding main ideas

Students often find it difficult to understand the difference between a main idea and a detail. Explain that a main idea is more than just a topic or subject. It includes the topic and an idea about that topic that the writer supports with details. The main idea is often (although not always) contained in the first paragraph of the reading. Sometimes it appears at the very beginning of the introductory paragraph, and sometimes at the end.

STRATEGY: Encourage students to get into the habit of finding and underlining the main idea sentence of every reading passage.

Additional activity

Before asking the students to complete exercise B, *Restating*, review the grammar of comparisons. Point out that in a comparative sentence, the word *far* means "a lot."

ANSWERS
Reading
2, 4, 5

After you read
A
a. 6   b. 5   c. 4   d. 3   e. 2
B
1. less   3. One-third   5. more   7. fewer
2. Twenty   4. more   6. few

Cultural notes

White-collar/blue-collar The terms *white-collar* and *blue-collar* come from the color of the shirts traditionally worn by male office workers and manual laborers. Traditionally, men working in offices wore white button-down shirts, suits, and ties, while men working as manual laborers often wore blue denim shirts or blue uniforms.

A, B, C student In the United States and Canada, students are usually graded with letters, rather than numbers. Possible grades include A, B, C, D, and F, with A corresponding to excellent work (90–100 percent), B corresponding to good (80–89 percent), C corresponding to fair (70–79 percent), D corresponding to poor but still passing (65–69 percent), and F corresponding to complete failure (0–64 percent).

READING 3   Pity the poor lottery winner

Pages 14-15

This reading presents the stories of some lottery winners.

Additional vocabulary

beg: ask for something in an urgent way
break into: enter a building illegally, especially to steal something
cheat: act in a way that is dishonest, especially to get something for yourself
family ties: relationships with family members
kidnap: illegally take a person away by force, usually in order to demand money in exchange for releasing them
no way: definitely not
pity: have sympathy and understanding for someone else's suffering or troubles

continued on next page

poor: deserving sympathy
right: your opportunity to act and to be treated in particular ways
threat: a statement that someone will be hurt or harmed, especially if they do not do something in particular
what is more: additionally; also

Understanding main ideas

See the Teaching suggestions for this skill on page 8.

ANSWERS

Reading

1, 3, 4, 6, 7, 8

After you read

A

1. not the main idea (The only paragraph that includes this perspective is the third one.)

2. not the main idea (The amount of money is a fact, not an idea.)

3. main idea (See the first two sentences of the reading for the main idea.)

4. not the main idea (Very few details are given about how the winners spent their money. Only paragraphs 2 and 3 mention how the money was spent.)

5. not in the text

B

1. William	3. William	5. Paul	7. William
2. Cindy	4. Paul	6. Cindy	8. William

WRAP-UP
Page 16

Additional vocabulary

owe: have to pay back money someone lent you

ANSWERS

Across

2. frugal
3. millionaires
7. win
8. debt
9. high
10. invest
11. earn
12. sue
13. fortune

Down

1. compulsive
2. financial
4. spend
5. wealthy
6. broke
10. inherit
12. save
14. own

Additional activity

Divide the class into groups of three to five students each, and have each group design and conduct a survey together. Ask them to organize the information they collect in a series of posters with charts or graphs that show the most common answers. During each class session (for as many groups as you have), ask one group to put up their posters on the wall of the classroom. Each student in the group should be responsible for explaining at least one poster. Tell the other students in the class to walk around, look at the posters, and ask questions. This presentation method works especially well for groups with members who are not comfortable speaking in front of a large group.

Page 17

Additional vocabulary

advancement: promotion to a higher level within a place of work
benefits: services given to an employee in addition to pay (for example, health insurance)
challenging: needing great mental or physical effort in order to be done successfully
flexible schedule: working hours that can be changed easily
job requirements: abilities or experiences needed for a job
poll: a study of a group's opinion on a subject, in which people are questioned and their answers examined; a survey
starting position: an entry-level job

Additional activity

Before students think of a job that they would like to have, use yourself as a model. Explain your current position, or a position you would like to have. This ensures that students understand the vocabulary before answering the questions.

READING 1 **Your first job**

Pages 18-19

This reading presents the experiences of several people who have just started working.

Additional vocabulary

above: at a higher level than
come and go: be hired for a job and then very quickly fired
deal with: manage
flip a mental switch: suddenly change your way of thinking
get by: manage in a difficult situation
groceries: the food you buy in a supermarket
keep you on: continue to employ you
pick up: get something from somewhere
put together: well-groomed and professional
treat: behave toward someone in a particular way

Making inferences

Sometimes students have a hard time making inferences because they don't notice a writer's tone. Help students understand that inferences are not blind guesses. Point out that they should decide whether a writer is using positive, negative, or neutral vocabulary. In this reading, for example, Peter, Jennifer, and Kelly tend to use negative words, so the tone is negative. Therefore, they probably didn't feel good about their first job. Jason and Adam used positive words, so the tone is positive. They felt good about their first job.

STRATEGY: When students work on an inference exercise, encourage them to pay attention to positive, negative, and neutral words.

ANSWERS
Reading

1. Adam	3. Jennifer	5. Lisa
2. Kate	4. Kelly	6. Peter

After you read

A

Not good: Peter, Jennifer, Kelly
Neutral: Lisa, Kate
Good: Jason, Adam

B

1. a	2. b	3. b	4. a	5. b	6. b

READING 2 Job satisfaction

Pages 20-21

This reading looks at the results of a poll on the subject of job satisfaction.

Additional vocabulary

corporate culture: the work environment that is specific to large business corporations

elsewhere: at another place

get in return: get something in exchange for something else

make a contribution: be an important part of a group effort

motivations: reasons for doing something

move up: get a better job

praise: express strong admiration for or approval of

rank at the top: have a position that is higher or more important than others

thrive: grow, develop, or be successful

ultimately: finally; in the end

work environment: the conditions that you work in, such as hours, safety, and benefits

Restating

Students sometimes find it difficult to recognize restatements. When students complete this type of exercise, ask them to explain how the two statements are similar or different. For example, the second statement might be opposite in meaning, too general or specific, or contain an opinion that is not expressed in the original statement.

Additional activity

Bring (or have students bring) copies of the help-wanted section of an English-language newspaper for at least half of your class. As a warm-up, have students work in pairs to find a job they would like to apply for. Ask them to explain to their partners why they find that job attractive. Tell them to use the results of the job satisfaction poll on page 20 as a guide.

ANSWERS
Scanning
1. Nature of the work and job satisfaction
2. Flexible schedule and work-life balance
3. Work environment and corporate culture
4. Advancement opportunity and personal growth
5. Salary and benefits

After you read
A
3. managers
B
1, 3, 6
C
1. D   2. S   3. S   4. S

READING 3   Are you a workaholic?
Pages 22-23

This reading describes compulsive workers and the problems they experience.

Additional vocabulary

abuse: use something in a harmful way
take as an insult: look at as a rude remark
be viewed: be looked at or considered by others
enrich: improve
equate: consider to be the same
get applauded for: be praised for
neglect: fail to give needed care or attention to something or someone
reinforce: influence behavior through rewards and punishments
self-medicate: try to cure your illness or problem without asking a doctor

subtle: not obvious or noticeable
take on: accept
work long hours: work more than the average number of hours

Guessing meaning from context

See Teaching suggestions for this skill on page 2.

Additional activity

To check students' comprehension of the distinction between a hard worker and a compulsive worker, ask them to write two paragraphs. In one, they should describe a compulsive worker, and in the other, a hard worker. They can describe people they know, or they can invent them. Then, have them exchange paragraphs with other students to see if their classmates can guess which describes the hard worker and which describes the workaholic. Give students the following guidelines for writing their paragraphs: What kind of work do they do? How many days/hours a week do they work? How much vacation time do they take? How much time do they spend with their family every week? What do they do in their free time?

ANSWERS
Reading
1, 2, 3, 4, 5

After you read
A
1. Do you think about work all the time? Do you work long hours, far beyond the requirements of the job? Are you anxious when you're not at work?
2. "Like other addictions, you are seeking a way of not having to look at or feel things or just to self-medicate to take care of pain, anxiety, or feelings."
3. Hard work enriches your life even if it includes some periods of long hours and extra work. Compulsive work, on the other hand, prevents you from leading a full life.
4. But we live in a society that rewards compulsive work, and we get applauded for keeping long hours and taking on more . . . responsibilities. ". . . Our society in some ways reinforces and rewards workaholism. Sometimes it's subtle, but there is a lot of recognition given to people for being extremely busy."
5. Being called a workaholic is often not taken as an insult, for example, like being accused of alcoholism.
6. The people who didn't work on Saturday and Sunday were viewed as less interested in their jobs.

B
Positive: applauded, enriches, recognition, rewards
Negative: abuse, anxious, insult, overwork, pain

ANSWERS

A

1. negative	3. neutral	5. positive	7. negative
2. positive	4. negative	6. positive	

B

1. dog-eat-dog	3. line of work	5. will go a long way
2. work like a dog	4. not pull your weight	6. up-and-coming

Additional activity

Games are an excellent way for students to review the unit vocabulary. Here is one suggestion:

1. Before class, prepare a set of 20 cards with one vocabulary word or expression from the unit written on each. Choose words or expressions that are easy to act out. The seven idioms from the vocabulary expansion lesson work well for this activity.

2. Divide the class into teams of three or four students each. Explain that you will show one person on each team the same word or expression. Then, he or she will have to mime (or act out) that word to get his or her teammates to guess the word. Remind students that the "actor" may not speak or write any words. The first team to guess the word gets a point. Then, assign another actor for each group.

4 Sports

PREVIEW

Page 25

Additional vocabulary

fan: a person who is very much interested in a sports team or entertainer
pro: short for *professional*; a person who receives money for playing a sport
victor: the winner of a competition
worth: deserving of; valued at

Additional activity

Bring in some baseball cards (or other types of sports cards or stickers). Pass them around, and ask students if they've heard of the players on the cards. Find out if anyone in the class has ever collected sports cards. Have the students discuss why people like to collect and trade sports cards, and why someone would pay a lot of money for a rare card. Assign a student to search the Internet to find out how much people are willing to pay for a rare sports card.

READING 1

Pages 26-27

Do pro athletes make too much money?

This reading focuses on whether professional athletes deserve so much money.

Additional vocabulary

event: a set of races or competitions
fraction: a very small part or amount of something
rate: an amount or level of payment
reflect: show, express, or be a sign of something
start out: begin one's career
willing: ready or eager to do something

Reading skill

Distinguishing arguments

Students sometimes confuse their own ideas with those presented in a text. To help them understand the difference between their own ideas and those of the writer, ask them to underline the sentences in the text that contain arguments.

STRATEGY: Encourage students to underline the sentences in the text that contain arguments. Then, if they make a mistake, you can ask them to tell you what they underlined in the text. They should realize they are wrong when they are unable to point to a sentence that contains their incorrect answer.

Reading

1. a basketball player
2. a baseball player
3. a hockey player
4. a football player
5. the president of the United States
6. a firefighter
7. a teacher
8. a new police officer

After you read

A

3. The article begins with facts. Then it explains the opinions of different groups of people.

B

1. b (a. Top athletes believe they are worth a lot of money because they make millions of dollars for team owners. c. Some also say that athletes are paid fairly when compared with others in the entertainment industry. It is not unusual for movie stars to make between $15 million and $20 million per movie. d. Sports fans are willing to pay increasingly high ticket prices and watch TV sports events in large numbers.)

2. a, d (b. Police officers, firefighters, and doctors save lives — sometimes while risking their own — for a fraction of what sports stars make. c. People who think pro athletes are overpaid say other, more important professions are more worthy.)

Cultural notes

Sports agents In the United States, professional athletes and others in the entertainment industry often hire agents to represent them in contract negotiations. It is a sports agent's job to get the best deal possible for an athlete (for example, salary, benefits, and length of contract). Agents are usually paid a percentage of the contract amount.

American football versus soccer What is known as football in most countries is called soccer in North America. In the United States, football is an entirely different game. Two teams of eleven players each move an oval ball along the field by running with it or throwing it. Points are scored by moving the ball across the line at the end of the field or by kicking it between two posts.

This reading explains the reasons for the increasing popularity of extreme sports.

Additional vocabulary

absence: lack of existence
affluence: the condition of having a lot of money or possessions
courage: the ability to control fear and deal with something dangerous, difficult, or unpleasant
display: show
ease: freedom from difficulty, effort, or pain
fit: in good physical condition, especially as a result of exercise
going rate: the amount that people are willing to pay for something at a particular time
have to do with: be related to
high-tech: short for *high technology*; using the most advanced machines and methods
relative: compared with something else
take part: participate
take up: begin to do something, especially a hobby or sport

Reading skill

Making inferences

Remind students to be careful when making inferences. A good example is exercise B, item 3: *People who have difficult lives are not interested in extreme sports.* In this text, the writer states that one of the reasons for the popularity of extreme sports is that people today live lives of "relative ease." Based on that information, it's reasonable to infer that people whose lives are *not difficult* might do extreme sports to add excitement to their lives. However, it's not valid to conclude that all people who have *difficult* lives *do not* take part in extreme sports.

ANSWERS
Reading
1, 4, 5, 8, 10, 11

After you read

A

1. don't fear
2. you are born with
3. an exciting
4. high
5. different from
6. more

B
1, 5, 6
(Statement 2 might be true, but it is just as probable that high-tech equipment simply makes extreme sports more comfortable. Statement 3 makes an assumption that may or may not be true. Statement 4 is incorrect because although young people do extreme sports, so do many older people.)

Cultural note

Sports psychology There are psychologists who specialize in very specific types of problems. Sports psychology is one specialization that is becoming popular. Some famous athletes who are having performance problems visit sports psychologists to get help. They hope that their performance will improve as a result.

READING 3
Pages 30-31 **Frequently asked questions about the ancient Olympic Games**

This reading presents information about the early Olympic Games.

Additional vocabulary

> **chariot:** a two-wheeled vehicle pulled by a horse, used in ancient times
> **equestrian:** connected with horseback riding
> **fine:** make someone pay money as a punishment for not obeying a rule or law
> **free-born:** not a slave
> **gym:** short for *gymnasium*; a large room designed and equipped for doing sports, physical training, and exercise
> **rivalries:** serious and often continuing competitions
> **set up:** place something in an upright position
> **wrestling:** a sport in which two competitors try to force each other to the ground

Reading skill

Understanding meaning from related forms

This type of exercise offers an opportunity to teach some basic word-form patterns. One pattern that appears in this exercise is shown below. Write this table on the board, and ask students to supply the missing information. All of the words appear in this unit. Explain that this rule will not work for all adjectives.

Word formation pattern	Rule	Example adjective	Example noun
Adjective into noun	add *-ness* to the end of some common adjectives to form nouns	fair	fairness
		bold	?
		fit	?
		courageous	?
		?	self-centeredness
		competitive	?
		rebellious	?

ANSWERS

Reading

1. Any free-born male Greek in the world could compete.
2. All of the judges came from Elis, the local region that included Olympia.
3. The Olympic winners received a crown made from olive leaves, and they could have a statue of themselves set up in Olympia.
4. The penalty for cheating was a fine.
5. Unmarried women could attend the Games, but married women could not. Women were not allowed to compete in the Games, but they could enter equestrian events as the owner of a chariot team or an individual horse.

After you read

A

1. athletic, d
2. division, f
3. strength, e
4. fame, b
5. expense, c
6. fairness, a

B

1. Religion and politics were part of the ancient Olympics.
2. Women did not compete in the ancient Olympics.
3. Married women were forbidden to attend the ancient Olympics, but unmarried women were allowed to attend.
4. Winners in the ancient Olympics received olive crowns as prizes.
5. Judges in the ancient Olympics came from the local region of Elis.
6. Anyone who cheated in the ancient Olympics had to pay a fine.

 WRAP-UP

Page 32

Additional vocabulary

club: a long, thin stick used to hit a golf ball

court: a rectangular area used for playing sports such as tennis

homerun: in baseball, when a player hits the ball and scores, usually by hitting the ball a long way

inning: one of nine periods of play in a baseball game

lane: a narrow section in a running track marked to keep the competitors apart

official: a person who is responsible for determining the winner in certain sports events

racket: an object consisting of a net fixed tightly to an oval frame with a long handle, used in sports such as tennis for hitting a ball

continued on next page

referee: a person who controls a game and makes sure the rules are followed

swing: cause something to move from one side to the other

tee: the place where you begin to hit a golf ball, or the small stick that holds the ball up so that you can hit it easily

track: the sport of competitive running or a wide circular path used for this sport

umpire: a person who controls a game and makes sure that the rules are followed

ANSWERS

A
1. baseball
2. basketball
3. golf
4. soccer (football in all countries except the United States)
5. tennis
6. track

B
1. ballpark, court, course, field, track
2. bat, basket, club, ball, tee, racket, net, running shoes
3. umpire, referee, official
4. homerun, point, basket, goal
5. catch, shoot, swing, kick, run
6. inning, game, hole, match, race

Additional activity

Bring in the sports section of an English-language newspaper before students complete the *Sports and you* activity. Ask students to compare sports news with that in their countries. Have them work in small groups to come up with a list of similarities and differences.

5 Weather

PREVIEW
Page 33

Additional vocabulary

equator: an imaginary line that goes around the middle of the earth and that is an equal distance from the North Pole and the South Pole
forecast: a statement of what is likely to happen in the future
keep an eye on: watch
meteorologist: a scientist who studies the earth's atmosphere and how it causes changes in weather conditions
natural disaster: an event in nature causing great harm, damage, or suffering

Additional activity

Before class, find out the temperature in several well-known cities around the world. Before beginning the preview questions, write the names of the cities on the board. Ask students to consider the latitude of each city and the time of year to make an educated guess (see definition below) about the temperature in each place. Write their guesses on the board, and then compare them to the actual temperatures.

ANSWERS

Places on the planet Earth: the North Pole, the South Pole, the equator
Weather problems: a hurricane, humidity, a flood, a storm, a tornado
Weather measurements: temperature, air pressure

READING 1
Pages 34-35
Keeping an eye on the weather

This reading presents information about how meteorologists predict the weather.

Additional vocabulary

educated guess: a guess that is made using judgment and knowledge
globe: the world
network: a group formed from parts that are connected together
pine cone: the hard, oval fruit of the pine tree
satellite: an artificial object sent up into space to travel around the earth
sophisticated: complicated

Understanding text organization

The use of pronouns and demonstratives (*this, that, these, those*) helps to give a text coherence.

STRATEGY: When students complete an exercise in understanding text organization, encourage them to underline the word each pronoun refers to.

ANSWERS

Reading
1, 2, 4

After you read

A

| 1. e | 2. d | 3. a | 4. f | 5. b | 6. c |

B

a. 7 (them = weather vanes)

b. 5 (It = flying directly into storms)

c. 3 (They = other satellites)

d. 9 (These = other stations)

e. 4 (They = radio transmitters)

f. 6 (This = the World Meteorological Organization)

READING 2 ## Nature's weather forecasters

Pages 36-37

This reading explains how changes in wildlife behavior can help us anticipate changes in the weather.

Additional vocabulary

chirp: make a short high sound

crab: a sea animal that has five pairs of legs and a round, flat body covered by a shell

drop: a change to a lower level

flock: a group of birds

huddle: come close together in a group, especially because of cold or fear

irritable: feeling annoyed or angry

mammal: any animal in which the female gives birth to babies, not eggs, and feeds them on milk from her own body

pound: hit repeatedly with force

seagull: a large bird that lives near salt water

sense: any of the five physical abilities to see, hear, smell, taste, and feel

sit out a storm: wait until a storm is over, usually in a safe place

squeak: make a short, very high sound

Understanding details

See the Teaching suggestions for this skill on page 3.

Additional activity

Bring in pictures of the animals and insects mentioned in the reading, as well as others that are commonly found in the area(s) where students live. Display them on the board or walls of the classroom with the name of the animal written below the picture so that students can refer to them as they read.

ANSWERS

Reading

1. come out of	4. come onto land	6. in large flocks
2. more	5. sit on the ground	7. more
3. come down from		

After you read

A

1. migrate	3. quarrelsome	5. seek shelter
2. reluctant	4. active	6. roost

B

1. T
2. ? (The reading doesn't mention drops in temperature, just drops in pressure.)
3. ? (The reading only mentions deer, but that doesn't mean that they are the only animals to behave this way.)
4. F (Not all animals seek shelter, just some. For instance, field mice come out of their holes, and cockroaches become more active.)
5. T

READING 3 Could you survive a natural disaster?

Pages 38-39

This reading gives practical advice on how to protect your home and family from natural disasters.

Additional vocabulary

basement: a part of a building that is below the level of the first floor
battery-operated: powered by a device that produces electricity
board up: cover (especially a window) with thin, flat pieces of wood
canned food: food that is packaged in a metal container
evacuate: remove people from a dangerous place
first-aid kit: a small box with bandages and medicine used for emergency medical treatment
get through: survive
jug: a large container for liquids with a handle and a narrow opening at the top
lawn furniture: tables and chairs that can be used outdoors
pick: choose
prescription drug: a medicine that can only be obtained with a doctor's written direction
safety deposit box: a strong box in a bank where you can keep valuable things

Understanding text organization

See the Teaching suggestions for this skill on page 24.

Additional activity

Bring a world map or a globe to class. Show different regions of the world and ask students to tell you which natural disasters mentioned in the reading occur in those parts of the world. Ask students to think of other natural disasters, and write these on the board. Examples of natural disasters not mentioned in the reading include tidal wave, mud slide, avalanche, typhoon, and forest fire.

ANSWERS

Reading
Answers may vary.

After you read

A

a. 5   b. 3   c. 1   d. 4   e. 2

B

1. tornado	5. earthquake
2. all disasters	6. hurricane, flood
3. hurricane, tornado, flood	7. earthquake
4. flood	8. hurricane, tornado, flood

WRAP-UP

Page 40

Additional vocabulary

can't stand: hate; strongly dislike
Celsius: a scale for measuring temperature in which water freezes at 0° and boils at 100°
coming days: days that are in the very near future
don't mind: not be bothered or annoyed by
erupt: explode, throwing out hot rocks and burning substances
Fahrenheit: a scale for measuring temperature in which water freezes at 32° and boils at 212°

ANSWERS

A

Adjective	Noun	Verb
1. active	action	act; activate
2. convertible	conversion	convert
3. equipped	equipment	equip

---

4. humid	humidity	humidify
5. migratory	migration	migrate
6. predictable	prediction	predict
7. quarrelsome	quarrel	quarrel
8. stormy	storm	storm

B

1. active (adj.)
2. stormy (adj.)
3. equipment (noun)
4. convert (verb)

5. migratory (adj.)
6. predict (verb)
7. humidity (noun)

Additional activity

Before having the students complete exercise A, review the function and common placement of nouns, verbs, and adjectives.

UNIT 6 Clothes

PREVIEW
Page 41

Additional vocabulary

casual: not formal; relaxed in style
conservative: traditional in color and style
fashion: a clothing style that is popular at a particular time or place
image: the way people think of someone or something
in: fashionable
out: unfashionable
outfit: a set of clothes worn for a particular occasion or activity
stylish: fashionable
trend: new development in clothing, etc.

Additional activity

Bring in photographs of your friends, family, or acquaintances. Make sure that their clothing is visible in the photographs. On the board, write the professions of the people in the photographs, and have students try to match the people to their professions. Have them explain their answers. This should lead naturally into a discussion about what people's clothing says about them.

READING 1
Pages 42-43

Dressing for success

This reading describes what clothes you should wear to a job interview.

Additional vocabulary

dress code: a particular way that people must dress in particular places or for particular events
expectation: the feeling or belief that something will or should happen
inappropriately: not done correctly for a particular situation
presenter: a speaker at a formal meeting
reputation: the general opinion that people have about someone or something
session: a formal meeting arranged for a particular activity
specialize: know a lot about a particular area or field

Guessing meaning from context

Point out that the contextual clues are often not found in the same sentence as the unfamiliar word. Students should get into the habit of reading the entire paragraph that contains the unfamiliar word or words. The target word *painful* (exercise A, item 1) illustrates this point. While the word appears in the first line of paragraph one, the first contextual clue (*a big mistake*) does not appear until line nine.

STRATEGY: Encourage students to look for and circle contextual clues in sentences that precede or follow the sentence in which the unfamiliar word occurs.

ANSWERS

Reading

The man is dressed appropriately for a job interview.

After you read

A

1. d	5. h
2. f	6. c
3. g	7. e
4. a	

B

1. F (In the end, she did not get a job offer.)
2. ? (The text only tells us that Sandra didn't get a job offer; it doesn't mention what happened to the other job candidates.)
3. F (Almost everyone else except Sandra was dressed conservatively.)
4. T
5. T
6. F (The dress code varies from company to company, as the example of David Lo illustrates.)
7. ? (The text only says that his strategy is smart; it doesn't say whether he got a job.)

Cultural note

Job interviews In many western countries, job interviews are a very important part of the hiring process. Some typical steps in the search for a professional position in the United States are as follows:

1. Candidates learn of an open position (often through a friend or acquaintance, the help-wanted section of a newspaper, a job search website, the job placement office at their university, or a professional journal or magazine).

2. Candidates submit a résumé or CV (curriculum vitae) outlining their educational and professional experience.

3. The personnel department of the organization where candidates are applying reviews their résumé. If they meet the job requirements, they are contacted and an interview is scheduled. Depending on the level of responsibility of the position, candidates may be interviewed several times, and by different members of the organization.

READING 2 — Casual dress in the workplace

This reading presents a trend in the United States toward dressing casually in the workplace.

Additional vocabulary

contributor: one of several reasons for something
controversial: causing or likely to cause disagreement
dress-down: wearing less-formal clothes than you usually wear
dressy: suitable for formal occasions
in style: fashionable
last: continue for a long period of time
slacks: a pair of pants
standards: the expected level of quality
wind down: end gradually or in stages

Reading skill

Distinguishing arguments

When students try to identify the arguments in a reading passage, they should look at key sentences containing positive or negative words. Exercise B on page 45 demonstrates this point very well. For example, in item 1, the positive expression *good mood* shows that this is an argument in favor of casual clothes. The negative words in item 3, *lowers an employer's professional image,* show that this is an argument against casual clothes.

STRATEGY: Encourage students to identify positive and negative words or expressions in key sentences of the reading.

ANSWERS

Reading
3. Some companies allow workers to wear casual clothes on Fridays. Not everybody is happy about this change.

After you read

A

1. atmosphere	3. retire	5. impress
2. embarrassing	4. formality	

B

1. for	3. against	5. against
2. for	4. against	

30   Unit 6 • Clothes

This reading argues in favor of requiring children to wear school uniforms.

Additional vocabulary

creativity: the ability to produce original and unusual ideas
design: make or draw plans (for something)
distract: take someone's attention away from what he or she is doing
engage: use
exclude: keep someone out
individuality: that which makes one person different from another
law and order: the condition of a society in which laws are obeyed
object: express opposition, dislike, or disapproval
symbol: a sign, shape, or object used to represent something else
tear down: destroy

Reading skill

Understanding main ideas

See the Teaching suggestions for this skill on page 8.

Additional activity

The topic of this reading is suitable for a class debate. Divide students into three teams: one in favor of school uniforms, one against school uniforms, and one team of judges. Make sure that the groups are sitting far enough apart so that they cannot hear each other. Tell the opposing teams to make a list of arguments that support their position, and then think of ways the opposing team will argue against them. They should also make a list of questions to ask the opposing team. Meanwhile, the team of judges should make a list of arguments that they expect to hear from both sides, and develop a list of questions to ask each team. Before the debate, make sure the students understand the rules, which will vary depending on class size, teacher preference, and class time. Here is a suggested set of rules:

1. Each team gets two minutes to make an opening statement. The order of the statements is determined by a coin toss.

2. The teams take turns asking questions for a set period of time (for example, 20 minutes in total, ten minutes each). The judges keep time, making sure that both teams ask an equal number of questions and speak for an equal amount of time.

3. The judges ask questions of both teams for a set period of time (for example, ten minutes in total, five minutes for each team).

4. Each team gets one minute to make a final statement. The order of the statements is determined by a coin toss.

5. The judges meet and decide on a winner.

6. The judges announce the winner, giving specific reasons for their decision.

Variation:
- You can be the judge, or judges can be brought in from the outside.

ANSWERS
Reading
1, 3
After you read
A
1. a   2. b   3. b   4. a
B
1. f   2. d   3. a   4. b

WRAP-UP
Page 48

Additional vocabulary

runway: a long, level platform or stage where fashion models walk in order to show clothes to an audience

---

ANSWERS
A
1. a, b, d
2. b
3. g, i, j
4. e, c
5. f, h
B
Answers may vary.

Additional activity

This vocabulary section provides an opportunity to present or review phrasal verbs. Have students complete exercise A in pairs, making sure they understand the meaning of each phrasal verb. Before beginning exercise B, discuss the answers to exercise A. Ask students to work on exercise B in pairs or small groups. Circulate to check their work.

PREVIEW
Page 49

Additional vocabulary

> **bewildered:** confused and uncertain
> **get along with:** have a good relationship with (someone)
> **journal:** a magazine or newspaper, especially one that deals with a
> specialized subject

Additional activity

When students finish the vocabulary exercise, divide them into groups of three or four. Ask them to choose one vocabulary item, and use it to tell the group about a cross-cultural experience they have had. Before they begin, describe one of your own cross-cultural experiences as a model. As they work, circulate to make sure they understand the vocabulary. To end the activity, ask the class to share one experience for each vocabulary item.

> ### ANSWERS
> *Positive*: mutual trust, relationship building, to respect
> *Negative*: bewildered, lack of interest, misunderstandings, rudeness
> *Neutral*: accustomed, different values

READING 1 **Adventures in India**
Pages 50-51

This reading contains diary entries of a student who spent a year in India.

Additional vocabulary

> **add up:** collect or increase gradually, especially over a period of time
> **be through:** experience (something), especially something unpleasant or
> difficult
> **distressing:** causing great mental or physical suffering
> **dread:** feel fear or anxiety about something that is going to happen or might
> happen
>
> *continued on next page*

fix in your memory: memorize something; do something to make sure you never forget

go by: pass, usually through a period of time

journey: a trip, especially over a long period or a great distance

know your way: be familiar with the route to a place

monsoon: the season of heavy rain that falls during the summer in hot Asian countries

overcome: unable to act or think in the usual way

relief: a feeling of happiness that something unpleasant has not happened or has ended

Reading skill

Understanding main ideas

Introduce students to the concepts of *general* and *specific*. Give examples of statements that are very general and very specific to illustrate why a particular statement is not a main idea. When they choose or write main idea sentences, tell them to identify incorrect answers as either *general* or *specific*.

ANSWERS

Reading
All the words should be checked.

After you read

A

1. a	2. a	3. b	4. a	5. b	6. b

B

1. positive	3. positive	5. positive and negative
2. negative	4. positive and negative	6. positive and negative

---

READING 2 · Body language in the United States

Pages 52-53

This reading describes appropriate body language in the United States.

Additional vocabulary

arm's length: a distance of approximately the length of one arm

curl: make a circular or curved shape

forearm: the lower part of the arm, between the wrist and the elbow

give up: allow (something) to be used by another person

index finger: the finger next to the thumb

scold: criticize angrily

twist: turn back and forth repeatedly

Guessing meaning from context

See the Teaching suggestions for this skill on page 2.

Additional activity

To introduce the concept of body language, ask a student to come to the front of the class. Start talking to him or her, and then gradually move closer, until the student becomes uncomfortable and begins to back away. Discuss what has happened with the class.

ANSWERS

Reading

a. 5   b. 1   c. 3   d. 4   e. 2

After you read

A

1. e   2. d   3. a   4. b   5. f   6. c

B

1, 5

READING 3 | Cross-cultural differences

Pages 54-55

This reading presents a British writer's observations on cross-cultural encounters.

Additional vocabulary

at the very least: if not worse
fall apart: fail completely
haste: great speed
lively: having or showing a lot of energy and enthusiasm
small talk: social conversation about unimportant things, often between people who do not know each other well
social: related to meeting and spending time with other people for pleasure

Recognizing audience

Before students identify the audience, ask them to look for words and phrases in the text that serve as clues about the types of audiences. For example, tell them to circle words that refer to people who want to learn about British culture, people who travel for their jobs, or students who take foreign language courses.

STRATEGY: Encourage students to circle any words in the text that are related to the audiences listed in the answer choices.

ANSWERS

Reading

1. Turkey
2. Turkey
3. Turkey
4. the U.K., France, and Spain
5. the U.K.
6. Germany

After you read

A

2. people who travel to different countries because of their jobs
   (Numbers 1 and 3 are incorrect because people who want to learn about British culture and college students are not mentioned in the article. Doing business in foreign countries, however, is mentioned numerous times.)

B

1. meet them for the first time
2. do something that confuses people
3. different
4. look at them as if you don't see them
5. tell you what to do
6. completely different
7. feel it is important

WRAP-UP

Page 56

ANSWERS

A

1. unable
2. unacceptable
3. unaware
4. uncomfortable
5. incomplete
6. inconvenient
7. incorrect
8. incredible
9. inexpensive
10. informal
11. unfriendly
12. unimportant
13. unknown
14. unnecessary
15. unspoken
16. unsuccessful

B

1. unfriendly
2. incomplete
3. inexpensive
4. unaware
5. unacceptable
6. inconvenient
7. uncomfortable
8. informal
9. unable

Additional activity

Understanding minor differences in meaning between two similar English words is challenging for many students. One way to help students understand these differences in meaning and use is to discuss the errors they make. After students complete exercise A, present the answers. Then have students work on exercise B in pairs or small groups. Using recent errors is a good way for students to learn to apply new vocabulary words to sentences. Circulate to check their work.

PREVIEW

Page 57

Additional vocabulary

asteroid: one of many rocky objects which circle the sun
cosmonaut: a Russian astronaut
far off: in the distant future
float: move easily through the air
outer space: the universe beyond the earth's atmosphere
weightless: not affected by gravity; having little or no weight
zero gravity: the condition of lacking any gravitational pull

Additional activity

Draw a diagram of our solar system on the board. Do not label the names of the planets. In a separate list, write the names of the planets, and see how many the students can label correctly on the diagram.

READING 1

Pages 58-59 ## Living in space

This reading explains some aspects of everyday life for astronauts living on a spacecraft.

Additional vocabulary

band: a thin, flat strip of a material put around something to fasten or strengthen it
clip: a usually metal or plastic object used for fastening things together or holding them in position
cylinder: a hollow tube with long straight sides and circular ends of equal size
elastic: able to stretch and be returned to its original shape or size
fasten: make or become firmly attached or closed
flow: move in one direction, especially continuously and easily
hose: a long, usually rubber or plastic pipe that can be bent and is used to move water or other substances
hygiene: the practice or principles of keeping yourself and your environment clean in order to maintain health and prevent disease
maintenance: the act of keeping something in good condition
press: push firmly against (something)

continued on next page

slippers: soft, comfortable shoes worn inside the house
strap: fasten something in position with a narrow piece of leather or other strong material

Reading skill

Making inferences

Explain that the strategies used to make inferences are very similar to those used to guess the meaning of unfamiliar words.

STRATEGY: Encourage students to look at the context and underline the sentences on which their inference is based, just as they do when they circle words and phrases for a *Guessing meaning from context* exercise.

Additional activity

To make sure students understand the vocabulary in this reading, ask them to label the illustrations with the appropriate words. For example, in the first illustration, students should label the picture with the words *cylinder, hose, clip,* and *soap-filled cloth.*

ANSWERS

Reading
1, 4, 6

After you read

A
2, 3

B
1. c   2. a   3. d   4. b

READING 2 **The planets**

Pages 60-61

This reading presents information about the planets in our solar system.

Additional vocabulary

cosmic: of or relating to the universe rather than to the earth alone
extinct: no longer active
lead: a dense, soft, dark gray metal
range: vary
rust: form a red-brown substance on the surface of iron and steel
scale: the size or level of something in comparison to what is average
sideways: (moving) from one side to the other, with a side to the front
sight: view

Using previous knowledge

Remind students to be careful not to let what they know interfere with their understanding of the information in the text. This is especially important when students read scientific or technical texts. It will help them recognize mistakes in the text and correct any misinformation that they have about the topic.

STRATEGY: Encourage students to check what they know or believe against what they read.

ANSWERS

Reading
1. T
2. F (Venus is actually very hot — 850° F, or 500° C.)
3. T
4. T
5. T
6. F (Saturn is the second-largest planet.)
7. F (Uranus is the third-largest planet. The largest is Jupiter.)
8. T
9. T

After you read

A
1. hard center
2. solid becomes liquid
3. turns around
4. special and important
5. small
6. different from

B
1. Mercury, Venus, Earth, Mars, Pluto
2. Pluto
3. Jupiter, Saturn, Uranus, Neptune
4. Mercury, Mars, Neptune, Pluto
5. Saturn, Uranus, Neptune
6. Jupiter, Saturn, Uranus, Neptune, Pluto
7. Mercury, Venus, Earth, Mars

READING 3 Space tours not so far off

Pages 62-63

This reading considers the possibility of space tourism in the future.

Additional vocabulary

fleet: a number of ships under the control of one company or organization
manned: with a person present in order to operate
pay good money: pay a lot of money
shift: the period that a person is scheduled to work
yacht: a large and usually expensive boat

Guessing meaning from context

This reading contains several key vocabulary items students might be familiar with, but that are used in ways that are likely to be unfamiliar. This is a good opportunity to stress the importance of using context, even with familiar words. Examples from this reading include *manned (man)*, *conclude*, *head*, and *ship*.

ANSWERS

Reading

1. People will start taking trips to outer space in 50 years.
2. A trip to outer space will cost $90,000, with a $6,000 deposit.
3. People aren't traveling to outer space now because of issues of expense, difficulty, and danger.
5. People will stay on space yachts, cruise lines, and eventually space hotels and resorts.
6. People will get oxygen and water at service stations located in hotels.

After you read

A

1. in 20 to 25 years	4. in 50 years
2. by 2030	5. by 2030
3. in 10 years; 10 years from now	

B

1. d   2. f   3. a   4. e   5. c   6. b

WRAP-UP
Page 64

ANSWERS

a. 6	c. 2	e. 11	g. 16
b. 4	d. 8	f. 15	h. 13

Additional activity

Concentration is a game that works well for reviewing technical or scientific terms. Here's the way it works:

1. Make a set of 20 large cards (large enough to be posted on the board and seen by all the students). Ten of the cards should have a vocabulary item written on one side, and the other ten should have the corresponding definitions of the ten items (one for each card).

2. Shuffle the cards well, and place them face down on the board in a pattern of five rows and four columns. When they are on the board in a regular pattern, number them from one to 20 (i.e., first row 1–4, second row 5–8, and so on).

3. Divide the class into teams of no more than four students each.

4. Ask a student from Team A to call out two numbers at random. Turn over the cards that the student has chosen, and give the students time to read what is on the cards. If the two cards match, and Team A recognizes that they match, remove the two cards from the board, and give them to Team A. Then, give Team A another turn. Proceed in the same fashion until Team A turns over two nonmatching cards. Then it is Team B's turn. Continue playing until all the cards have been removed from the board. The team with the most cards wins.

9 Animals

Page 65

Additional vocabulary

destructive: causing damage
exotic: unusual and often exciting because of coming from a distant country
poisonous: causing illness or death if swallowed, absorbed, or breathed
predator: an animal that hunts and kills other animals for food
species: a set of animals or plants with similar characteristics
take over: get control of something

Additional activity

Bring in pictures or drawings of the animals listed. Display them on the board or walls of the classroom with the name of the animal written below the picture so that students can refer to them as they complete the exercise.

POSSIBLE ANSWERS
1. alligators, bears, crocodiles, monkeys
2. frogs, insects, lizards, snakes
3. crocodiles, some species of turtles
4. alligators, crocodiles, snakes
5. no

READING 1 **The terrible toads**

Pages 66-67

This reading describes a plan to control insects by importing a species of toad.

Additional vocabulary

amphibian: a type of animal that lives both on land and on water
be in for: get or receive something unexpected
be (still) going strong: something that has existed for a long time, is successful and continues to work well
cane: the long hollow plant stems from which sugar is extracted
crop: a plant grown in large amounts by farmers, or the total amount gathered of such a plant

ecology: the relationship of living things to their environment and to each other, or the scientific study of this
field: an area of land with plants or crops growing on it
flesh: the meat of animals
on sight: as soon as you see something
plantation: a large farm on which a particular crop is grown
spray: a mass of very small drops of liquid forced through the air
squirt: quickly force (a liquid) out of something

Reading skill

Recognizing similarity in meaning

To help students recognize synonyms in a text, remind them to pay special attention to the use of examples. In this reading, for example, the word insect (probably a familiar word for students) appears in the main idea, while its synonym pest (probably a new word for students) is in a supporting sentence.

STRATEGY: As a way of identifying words that have similar meanings, encourage students to circle words or phrases that are used as examples. If they find an unfamiliar word in a supporting sentence, its synonym may be in the main idea. If the unfamiliar word is in the main idea, its synonym may be found in a supporting sentence.

ANSWERS					
Reading					
1, 2, 5, 6					
After you read					
A					
a. 4	b. 5	c. 1	d. 6	e. 2	f. 3
B					
1. d	2. a	3. b	4. c	5. a	6. e

READING 2 Exotic animals — not as pets!

Pages 68-69

This reading explains why keeping wild animals as pets is not a very good idea.

Additional vocabulary

branch: one of the offices or groups that form part of a large business organization
check out: find out if something is true
cramped: limited in the freedom to move because there is not enough space
fit: be the right size or shape

continued on next page

habitat: the natural surroundings in which an animal or plant usually lives

lecture: talk seriously in order to advise and criticize

let alone: not to mention; much less

poor: of a very low quality or standard; not good

preserve: an area of land kept in its natural state, for hunting and fishing or for raising animals or fish

recover: find or get back

scar: a mark left on the skin by a cut or burn that has healed

stick: put (something) somewhere, usually temporarily

take in: provide shelter

Reading skill

Making inferences

See the Teaching suggestions for this skill on page 38.

ANSWERS

Reading

1, 3, 5

After you read

A

a. 2	b. 4	c. 3	d. 1	

B

1. b	2. b	3. a	4. a	5. b

READING 3 Let's abandon zoos

Pages 70-71

This reading argues against the existence of zoos.

Additional vocabulary

decent: acceptable, satisfactory, or reasonable

enclosure: an area surrounded by a fence or other structure in order to be kept separate from other areas

range: the region a type of animal comes from and is most often found in

the wild: places that have few towns or roads, are difficult to get to, and lack conveniences

Distinguishing fact from opinion

Learning to distinguish fact from opinion is an important skill for students who need to read and research academic topics in English. Teach students to recognize positive or negative words that give a text its tone. Remind them to think about whether the information presented in the article can be proven. Exercise B is a good opportunity to practice this skill. As an example, point out that while it is possible to measure the size of cages in zoos to prove that they are smaller than the animals' natural habitats, it is not possible to prove that an animal is bored, since feelings are subjective.

ANSWERS

Reading

Checking predictions: 1. negative   3. positive   5. negative   7. negative
2. positive   4. positive   6. negative   8. negative

Writer's opinion: 2. The writer thinks it is wrong to keep animals in zoos.

After you read

A

1. b   2. b   3. b   4. a   5. b   6. a

B

1. opinion (The strongly negative first sentence gives an emotional, opinionated tone to the entire reading.)

2. opinion (The author does not support this claim with facts. It's impossible to know what an animal thinks, so how can we know if it feels bored or lonely? The strongly negative words — *captivity, bored, cramped, lonely, far from their natural homes* — indicate that this sentence expresses an opinion, not a fact.)

3. fact (It is possible to measure a cage and prove that it is small. It is also possible to read labels and record the type of information they contain.)

4. fact (The reference to the results of a worldwide study makes it clear that this sentence contains facts, and not just the author's opinion.)

5. fact (The reference to specific data indicates that this sentence contains facts.)

6. opinion (The use of *only if* in this sentence is a clue that it expresses an opinion, and not a fact. Is there really only *one* way to save an endangered species?)

WRAP-UP

Page 72

Additional vocabulary

associate: think about (something) as being connected to something else
sly: secretive, by hiding true opinions or intentions, or dishonest
stubborn: opposed to change or suggestion

ANSWERS

A

1. (be) in the doghouse
2. Hold your horses!
3. eat like a horse.

4. (be) a copycat
5. It's raining cats and dogs.
6. fight like cats and dogs

B

1. am in the doghouse
2. It's raining cats and dogs
3. Hold your horses

4. fight like cats and dogs
5. eat like a horse

Additional activity

Have students work in pairs or small groups to prepare a short skit illustrating one of the idioms. Their skits can be presented silently or using dialog. Tell students not to simply recreate the pictured situations. When they are ready, ask them to come to the front of the room and perform their skits for the other students. The class should be able to guess which idiom they are illustrating.

PREVIEW
Page 73

Additional vocabulary

natural wonders: beauty or surroundings that people greatly admire
rain forest: a forest in a hot area of the world that receives a lot of rain
scenic: having or showing beautiful natural surroundings

Additional activity

Bring a variety of travel brochures to class. (It is preferable that they be in English.) Allow students enough time to briefly look at the different types of destinations described in the brochures. Write these categories on the board: families with young children, singles, newlyweds, senior citizens, and college students. Then have students divide the destinations according to the type of person they think the vacation best suits. Ask them to explain their reasons.

READING 1 **Adventure travel**
Pages 74-75

This reading suggests some interesting travel destinations.

Additional vocabulary

charming: having a special quality that makes someone or something attractive
complex: a group of buildings that have a related or similar use
manor house: a large house in the country that has a large piece of land surrounding it
mule trails: a path through the countryside that mules use for transporting things
orchard: an area of land where fruit trees are grown
pagoda: a building used for religious worship in Asia; each floor has its own curved and decorated roof
sip: drink slowly by taking in small amounts at a time
situated: located; in a particular place
steep: rising or falling at a sharp angle
trek: a long, difficult walk over rough land
tunnel: a long passage under or through the earth
vineyard: a piece of land on which vines that produce grapes are grown

Understanding details

To find out how much information students retain from a reading, have them try to complete exercises from memory. Exercise A provides a chance for students to practice this skill. Ask them to find the mistake in each statement without referring back to the text. Then encourage them to recall the correct information before using the text to confirm their answers.

ANSWERS

Reading

1. Ecuador   2. France   3. Morocco   4. Vietnam

After you read

A

1. The travelers in Morocco spend most of their time in *the mountains*.
2. During the trip to Morocco, mules carry the *baggage*.
3. Travelers to Vietnam travel by *bicycle* around the country during some of the trip.
4. Divers around the Galapagos Islands can see *sea* lions and sea turtles.
5. Travelers to the Loire Valley take a tour of several of the most famous *chateaux*.

B

1. France   3. Morocco, Vietnam   5. Vietnam, France
2. Morocco, Ecuador   4. Morocco, Vietnam

READING 2 Choosing an ecodestination

Pages 76-77

This reading describes travel destinations that seek to preserve the environment.

Additional vocabulary

ecoresort: a resort that causes minimal harm to the environment
hospitality: kindness and special behavior, especially to guests
landscape: a large area of countryside
retire: go somewhere quiet or private, usually to rest
weave: make threads into cloth, a net, or a basket

Making inferences

See the Teaching suggestions for this skill on page 13.

Additional activity

Have students defend their answers to exercise B by giving specific reasons why they did *not* choose 1, 4, and 5. Ask them to start their answers with "*X* would not enjoy going to an ecodestination because. . ."

ANSWERS
Reading
1, 2, 4, 5
After you read
A
1, 4, 5
B
2, 3, 6

READING 3 **Jet lag**
Pages 78-79
This reading explains how long-distance travel affects the human body.

Reading skill
Guessing meaning from context

Exercise A illustrates specific techniques that will make it easier for students to understand the meaning of unfamiliar words based on context and personal experience. In item 4, the explanation after the target word *consciously* (par. 3) includes "homesick" and "wish for their own bed." These are feelings that students have probably experienced. More clues can be found in the explanation after the opposite of the target word, *unconsciously* (par. 3), including missing "the familiar timing of sunrise and sunset." These are feelings that students are less likely to have experienced.

STRATEGY: Encourage students to pay close attention to examples or explanations that follow unfamiliar words, and to prefixes that change the meaning of a word from positive to negative (i.e., *in-*, *im-*, *ir-*, *il-*, and *un-*).

ANSWERS
Reading
2. why people get jet lag
After you read
A
1. b   2. a   3. b   4. b   5. b   6. b   7. a
B
Possible answers:
1. travel a long distance in an east/west direction to a new time zone . . . sense of place . . . sense of time . . . sense of well-being
2. sense of time . . . sense of place . . . they could only travel very slowly, so they had time to adjust to changes in time and place
Paragraph 1 best summarizes the text.

POSSIBLE ANSWERS

A

1. a bathing suit, get sunburned, get a suntan, go fishing, go sightseeing, swimming/swim, a guidebook, sunbathe, suntan lotion, take lots of pictures; *added word*: swimming pool
2. a chair lift, get a suntan, get sunburned, go skiing/ski, a guidebook, lodge, skis, suntan lotion, take lots of pictures; *added word*: hot cocoa
3. get a suntan, get sunburned, go hiking/hike, go sightseeing, a guidebook, suntan lotion, take lots of pictures, a tour guide; *added word*: souvenir
4. get a suntan, get sunburned, go fishing, swimming/swim, lodge, suntan lotion, take lots of pictures, a tent; *added word*: mosquitoes

B

Answers may vary.

Additional activity

To practice vocabulary from the unit, have students work in pairs to role play a scene between a travel agent and a customer. Before beginning, tell the class to brainstorm a list of questions that travel agents usually ask their clients before designing their vacation. Students should also consider the types of questions that travelers ask their travel agents. Supply travel brochures for students to use to make the performances more realistic.

PREVIEW
Page 81

Additional vocabulary

not think much of: have a low opinion of
romance: a close relationship between two people who are in love with each other

Additional activity

Bring copies of personal ads from an English-language newspaper, magazine, or website to class. Have students discuss the similarities and/or differences between the ads.

Cultural note

Matchmaking service A matchmaker is a person who introduces one person to another in an attempt to help them form a relationship. In some societies, matchmakers are paid by families to search for suitable husbands or wives. In recent years, many agencies, especially Internet businesses, have been formed to help individuals find romantic relationships and marriage.

READING 1
Pages 82-83
Love on the Internet

This reading describes how people use the Internet to find a mate.

Additional vocabulary

anonymity: the state of being unknown
be dedicated to: exist completely for a particular purpose
chemistry: understanding and attraction between two people
go nuts: go crazy
golden boy: a young man who is very successful or promising
proposal: an offer of marriage
site: a website
spouse: a husband or wife

Relating reading to personal experience

Bring in some personal ads and read them aloud to the class. Then, ask students to write their own personal ads. Make sure that they include information about themselves and the kind of person they want to meet. Remind them that other students will read their ads. After you collect the ads, hang them in the classroom or read them aloud. Have students guess who wrote each one.

ANSWERS
Reading
3, 4, 5, 6

After you read

A
London . . . California . . . 27 years . . . Matrimonial Link . . .
Juliana Gidwani . . . 26 years . . . India . . . the United States . . .
Her parents . . . A1 Indian Matrimonials

B
1, 2, 3, 5

Cultural Note

Silicon Valley Silicon Valley is a residential and business area in California, between San Francisco and Los Angeles. It has a high concentration of computer companies that employ many young, single men. There are many more single men than single women, so young men living and working in Silicon Valley often complain that it is hard to find mates. Silicon Valley is named for the material silicon, which is used to make computer chips.

READING 2 Help on the Internet

Pages 84-85

This reading tells a true story of how the Internet saved a girl's life.

Additional vocabulary

chat room: a website where people "talk" to one another online through written conversations
on the way: happening or arriving soon
proper: correct for the situation
take seriously: give your complete attention

Understanding a sequence of events

Instead of writing the sequencing in their books, students can complete it orally.

1. Give each student one sentence from exercise A to memorize.

2. In random order, ask students to say their sentences out loud.

3. Tell them to get up and stand next to the students that have the sentences before and after theirs.

4. When students are satisfied with the sequence of the sentences, have them recite the story from the beginning.

5. Have them write it down from memory.

Note: If you have more students than sentences, divide the class into groups of ten students. You can also assign more than one student to memorize each sentence, making sure the two students sit and work together when it is time to repeat the sentences aloud. If you have fewer students than sentences, have some students memorize more than one sentence.

STRATEGY: Encourage students to circle the words that help them decide the order in which events happened.

ANSWERS
Reading
Answers may vary.
After you read
A

a. 7	c. 1	e. 9	g. 8	i. 2
b. 6	d. 3	f. 5	h. 4	j. 10

B

1. At first, Sean *didn't believe* the person sending the message for help was really sick.
2. Susan Hicks *was* Taija Laitinen.
3. Susan was in a chat room that day to *look for help*.
4. Susan didn't phone for help because there was no telephone *nearby and she couldn't move*.
5. Sean *knew* help was coming before Susan told him help had arrived.
6. Susan got medical treatment for an illness that was *very* serious.

Count me out

This reading presents one writer's opinion of the Internet.

Additional vocabulary

> **ad:** short for *advertisement;* a paid notice that tells people about a product or service
>
> **access:** the opportunity or ability to use (something)
>
> **age:** a particular period in time
>
> **bit:** part or piece
>
> **by no means all:** not complete; not everything
>
> **earthworm:** a common type of worm that moves through the earth
>
> **fellow human:** another person
>
> **key:** the most important part of achieving something
>
> **marvel:** something very surprising or admirable
>
> **world-shaking:** so important that it changes the world

Reading skill

Recognizing tone

Recognizing sarcasm in a text can be challenging. First, explain to students that sarcasm is often used to criticize someone or something in a way that is amusing. Make sure students understand that when something is *sarcastic*, it means the opposite of what it says. Then, have them underline places in the text that led them to their answer for exercise A.

STRATEGY: Encourage students to underline places in the text that lead them to the correct answer and to look for other examples of sarcastic language.

> ## ANSWERS
> ### Reading
> 3. The writer can live without the Internet.
>
> ### After you read
> **A**
> 3. sarcastic
>   (The following sentences are sarcastic in tone: par. 2: . . . if the matter was of world-shaking importance, over the telephone; par. 2: Then you spoke to a fellow human . . .; par. 4: There are, I am told, certain advantages in having access to the latest marvel of the age . . .; par. 5: More amazing things are yet to come . . .; par. 6: . . . I would like a gadget that not only thinks for me but also accepts responsibility for all my mistakes.)
>
> **B**
> 1. complex   2. gadget   3. attitude   4. old-fashioned   5. cure

C

1. People communicated with each other by writing letters or talking on the telephone.
2. He thought it was wrong that the cure was only available to those who have computers.
3. People use the Internet to pay bills, order groceries, or discuss illnesses with their doctor. They may also send love messages or get married.
4. In the future, the Internet may develop consciousness.
5. He would like a computer that thinks for him and takes responsibility for his mistakes.

WRAP-UP

Page 88

ANSWERS

A

1. c	2. d	3. j	4. b	5. f	6. e

B

1. turn to	3. turn out	5. get out of
2. sign off	4. log on	6. Count me out

Additional activity

This vocabulary section provides an opportunity to present or review phrasal verbs. Have students complete exercise A in pairs, making sure they understand the meaning of each phrasal verb. Before beginning exercise B, discuss the answers to exercise A. Ask students to work on exercise B in pairs or small groups. Circulate to check their work.

12 Friends

PREVIEW
Page 89

Additional vocabulary

caring: kind and considerate of people's feelings
commitment: a promise to give yourself, your time, your money, and so on, to support someone else
intimacy: a state of being a close personal friend or having a close, personal relationship
loyalty: the act of always being supportive
supportive: giving help and encouragement

Additional activity

Using the class results of the chart on page 89, tell students to count the number of responses for each category and then calculate these numbers into percentages. Write the results on the board, and discuss them. You can also have students use this survey with students from other classes, and then present the results. Another option is to compare the responses of male and female students.

READING 1
Pages 90-91

Ten easy ways to make friends

This reading presents some advice for making friends.

Additional vocabulary

this alone: just this thing, and nothing else

Reading skill

Predicting

Instead of students completing the predicting exercise individually, have them work as a class. Before they read, write the students' predictions on the board. After they finish reading, ask a student to come to the board and check (✓) the advice that appeared in the reading, and add any that is missing.

Reading
Answers may vary.

After you read

A

a. 4	c. 5	e. 9	g. 8	i. 6
b. 2	d. 10	f. 1	h. 3	j. 7

B

1. meet
2. watch it
3. copy it
4. good
5. the same way
6. have a good opinion of
7. nice to

READING 2 Best friends

Pages 92-93

This reading describes what it means to be a best friend.

Additional vocabulary

brutally: in a plain and direct way

fill (someone's) need: give (someone) what they want or need

flat tire: a tire (of a car) that has lost its air

give (someone) a kick in the pants: tell (someone) that they are acting badly and should improve their behavior

nonjudgemental: not forming opinions too quickly; not critical (of others)

play into: have an effect on (someone or something)

put it: express something with words, either orally or in writing

sorrow: a feeling of great sadness or regret

tow truck: a truck that has special equipment for pulling vehicles that cannot be driven

trustworthy: deserving of trust, or able to be trusted

unconditional: complete and not limited

Reading skill

Distinguishing main and supporting ideas

Ask students to give their answers to exercise B. If students think a statement is a main idea, ask them to find information to support that idea. If students think a statement is supporting information, ask them to find the main idea the information supports.

Additional activity

Ask students to bring a photograph of their best friend to class. Have them complete exercise C in small groups. As they discuss the questions, they can pass around their photographs.

READING 3 The new family

Pages 94-95

This reading explains why friends are becoming more important than family.

Additional vocabulary

former: of an earlier time, but not now
have more to do with: know more about and be more involved in
spare: not being used; extra
split up: end a relationship
spread far and wide: living in many different places
up to date: having the most recent information

Reading skill

Understanding reference words

Point out that the closest noun to the reference word is sometimes, but not always, the noun the reference word has replaced. For example, in item 4 of exercise A, the closest possessive noun to the possessive adjective *her* is *Erika's*. However, in item 6, the closest plural noun to the pronoun *them* is *parents*, which is not the answer.

STRATEGY: Encourage students to check their understanding of reference words by making sure the sentence still makes sense when they replace the reference word with the noun it refers to.

2. *Friends* (an American TV show)
3. *Real Women*'s (a TV show)
4. Erika's
5. Erika
6. friends

B
1. b   2. a   3. c

WRAP-UP
Page 96

ANSWERS

A

Adjective	Noun	Verb
1. advisable	advice	advise
2. confident	confidence	confide
3. consistent	consistency	consist
4. critical	criticism; critic	criticize
5. dependable	dependence	depend
6. imitative; imitation	imitation	imitate
7. judgmental	judgment; judge	judge
8. supportive	support	support

B
1. advise (verb)   6. criticize (verb)
2. consistent (adj.)   7. dependable (adj.)
3. judge (verb)   8. support (noun)
4. imitate (verb)   9. confident (adj.)
5. explain (verb)

Additional activity

Remind students that in English, some words with the same spelling and pronunciation can function as two different parts of speech. Some examples from exercise A are *judge* (verb or noun), *support* (verb or noun), and *imitation* (noun or adjective). Words that can be verbs or nouns are the most common. Explain that the only way to tell the difference is to check the sentence in which the word appears. Have students reread the first two paragraphs of the text on page 94 and see how many words they can find that can be used as both nouns and verbs. Then, ask them to label how the words are used in the reading: *N* for nouns and *V* for verbs.

Answers: ring (V), guess (V), time (N), call (V), split (V), start (V), spread (V), end (V), trust (N), talk (V)

UNIT 13 Gifts

PREVIEW
Page 97

Additional vocabulary

anniversary: a day on which an important event happened in a previous year, often a wedding
extravagant: very expensive
hard to please: difficult to make happy or satisfy
occasion: an event that occurs at a particular time
recipient: a person who receives something
sacrifice: give up something you want or need

Additional activity

Bring in a gift that is very special to you. Ask students to guess who gave it to you, and what the occasion was. Then tell them about it.

READING 1 Gift giving
Pages 98-99

This reading explains the meaning of gift giving in western cultures.

Additional vocabulary

a means of: a way of
aspect: a particular feature of or way of thinking about something
commercialism: the methods used to advertise and sell goods and services
confirm: make certain or fixed
highly: very
industrialized: having a lot of industry, including companies and factories
lie behind (something): cause (something)
reason alone: enough of a reason
ritual: a set of actions or words performed in a regular way, often as part of a ceremony

Reading skill

Relating reading to personal experience

Before students answer exercise C, have them write about one gift they received that they particularly liked and one that they didn't like. Tell students that others will read their work. Collect their papers. Redistribute the papers so that students now have the paper written by another student. Ask the class to find the person whose writing they have.

READING 2 | Modern day self-sacrifice

Pages 100-101

This reading tells the true story of a very special gift.

Additional vocabulary

astonished: very surprised

barely: by very little; almost not

bow: a knot with two loose ends used as a decoration

dawn on (someone): become known or obvious (to someone), often suddenly

goodies: something pleasant to eat

hardly: barely

helmet: a hard hat that covers and protects the head

keyboard: a musical instrument having keys like a piano

long-standing: having existed for a long period of time

restore: return (something) to an earlier condition

thrilled: extremely pleased

upon: soon or immediately after

Reading skill

Understanding a sequence of events

See the Teaching suggestions for this skill on page 53.

Additional activity

Bring several examples of advice columns from English-language newspapers, magazines, or websites to class. Ask students to compare the advice columns to those in their countries. Are there any similarities? Differences? For example, what kinds of problems do people write about for advice? What kinds of advice do the columnists give? Do most people write anonymously?

Reading

Answers may vary.

After you read

A

a. 7	c. 6	e. 3	g. 5
b. 2	d. 4	f. 1	

B

1. b	2. b	3. a	4. a	5. b

READING 3 **Gifts for the hard to please**

Pages 102-103

This reading describes some unusual gifts from a popular store.

Additional vocabulary

barometric: measuring air pressure

discreet: not attracting a lot of attention

drift away: fall asleep gradually and gently

enchanting: greatly charming or pleasing

flip-up: able to be moved by making a short, quick motion

motion sensor: a device that can detect small movements

multifunctional: having a variety of uses

outlet: a device connected to the wall to supply electricity

snooze: sleep lightly for a short time

strike your fancy: attract your attention and make you like something

ultra: extremely; very

warranty: a written promise by a company to repair or replace a product within a fixed period of time

Reading skill

Understanding details

Remind students that they shouldn't read the whole text again when they answer detail questions. Instead, suggest that they write the question number next to the place in the text where the answer is located. That way, they can refer back to the text more easily when explaining their answers to you or to other students.

Additional activity

Descriptions of practical devices often contain many prepositions, especially prepositions of movement, direction, and location. Photocopy the text on page 102 and replace all the prepositions with blank spaces. Then have students fill in the blanks with the appropriate prepositions.

ANSWERS

Reading

Talking Travel Companion®: 3, 5, 7, 9
Color Flow™ Light Show: 1, 2, 4, 8
Personal Warm+Cool System™: 6, 10

After you read

A

3. a catalog

B

1. in a hotel room
2. in a darkened room
3. turn the dial to select the temperature you want
4. not given
5. *Talking* Travel Companion®, Personal Warm+Cool System™
6. not given
7. not given
8. around your neck

WRAP-UP

Page 104

ANSWERS

a. 3   c. 6   e. 5   g. 8   i. 11
b. 2   d. 4   f. 10   h. 13

Reading skill

Using a dictionary

When discussing this exercise, remind students that dictionaries contain much more than just definitions. The example sentences, for instance, often include a lot of information about how to use the words, including prepositions or any other words that are commonly used with the target word.

STRATEGY: Encourage students to pay close attention to the grammar information and the examples found in many dictionary entries.

PREVIEW
Page 105

Additional vocabulary

envy: wanting something another person has
grief: very great sadness, especially at the death of someone
insecure: lacking confidence and doubtful about your own abilities
jealous: unhappy and slightly angry because you want someone else's
  qualities, advantages, or success; envious
not necessarily: not in all cases
resentment: anger or unhappiness because you have been hurt or not
treated fairly
tense: nervous, anxious, or unable to relax

Additional activity

To practice the new vocabulary, write the ranking system below on the board.
For each emotion, ask students to rank how often they experience it, from
1 (frequently) to 4 (never). Then, have them share their responses with a partner.

   1 = an emotion that they frequently experience

   2 = an emotion that they sometimes experience

   3 = an emotion that they rarely experience

   4 = an emotion that they never experience

ANSWERS

Nouns: anger, envy, fear, grief, resentment, shock, stress, tension

Adjectives: angry, embarrassed, envious, frustrated, insecure, jealous, lonely,
powerless, stressed, tense, upset

READING 1 **Jokes can't always make you laugh**

Pages 106-107

This reading explains what it means to have a sense of humor.

Additional vocabulary

> **awareness:** knowledge
> **bulletin:** a short piece of news on television or radio
> **central nervous system:** the brain and all the nerves in the body that make movement and feeling possible
> **crib:** a baby's bed with high sides
> **delivery:** the manner in which someone speaks, especially in public
> **element:** a part of something
> **inborn:** from birth
> **timing:** the ability to choose the right moment to do or say something
> **virtually:** almost

Reading skill

Guessing meaning from context

Remind students that contextual clues are often not found in the same sentence as the unfamiliar word. Students should get into the habit of reading the entire paragraph that contains the unfamiliar word or words. Exercise A illustrates this point. While the target word *heal* appears in the second sentence of paragraph 1, the first contextual clues, *important* and *positive*, don't appear until the next sentence.

Additional activity

Bring copies of comic strips from an English-language newspaper to class. Have students read them in pairs. As a class, discuss the ways that humor is different or similar from country to country. If you have time, another option is to remove or cover the dialog from the comic strip, then ask students to write in their own captions. Finally, pass around the originals and let students compare their jokes to the originals.

ANSWERS
Reading

| 1. a | 2. b | 3. b | 4. b | 5. a |

After you read
A

| 1. b | 2. b | 3. a | 4. a | 5. b | 6. b |

continued on next page

B
1. Humor and laughter can heal us physically, mentally, emotionally, and spiritually.
2. The capacity to laugh and smile is virtually inborn. The parts of the brain and central nervous system that control laughing and smiling are mature at birth in human infants.
3. People can develop a sense of humor by losing their inhibitions and learning to laugh at themselves.
4. Many people think that they do not have a good sense of humor because they are not good joke tellers.
5. The writer defines a sense of humor as "the ability to see the nonserious element in a situation."

READING 2 Envy: Is it hurting or helping you?

Pages 108-109

This reading describes the causes of envy and how to deal with it.

Additional vocabulary

as long as: only if
blurt out: say (something) suddenly and without thinking of the results
get rid of: free (a person or place) of something unwanted or harmful
guilty: feeling you have done something wrong
mean: unkind or not caring
nasty: mean, unpleasant, or offensive
remark: a spoken statement of an opinion or thought
take over: get control of something
think straight: think clearly
turn into: change one thing into something else
ultimate: final
work out: happen or develop in a satisfactory or successful way

Reading skill

Recognizing sources

When you discuss exercise A, ask students to consider all the choices very carefully. For example, this reading doesn't contain any "news," so it probably didn't come from the front page of a newspaper. It also doesn't contain a lot of scientific or academic terms, so it probably didn't come from a psychology textbook. Point out that the examples in the reading are all *women's* personal experiences, so a women's magazine is the most likely source.

STRATEGY: Encourage students to eliminate incorrect answers and explain why these choices are not correct.

Reading

1, 2, 3, 4

After you read

A

1. a women's magazine

B

1. b   2. a   3. a   4. b   5. a   6. a

C

1. It is *perfectly* normal to feel envy.
2. Envy is something that *all* people feel.
3. Envy can teach you a lot about *yourself*.
4. Envy makes you feel *bad* about yourself.
5. When you feel envy, you should ask yourself *why* you are feeling it.
6. If you want to get rid of your envy, it's good to have goals that seem *possible* to achieve.

READING 3 | The value of tears

Pages 110-111

This reading explains the reasons we cry and why crying can be good for us.

Additional vocabulary

bring on: cause
escape mechanism: a way of avoiding something difficult or painful
film: a thin layer of something on something else
hold back: stop (something) from happening
infection: a disease caused by bacteria or viruses
release: free (something or someone)
relieve: make something (bad or painful) less severe
runny nose: a nose that produces a lot of liquid
shed tears: cry
substance: a material with particular physical characteristics
suffer: experience or show the effects of (something bad)
therapy: treatment to help someone feel better or grow stronger, especially after an illness or emotional problem

Restating and making inferences

It is not always easy for students to recognize restatements and inferences. When the students practice this skill, ask them to refer directly to the relevant sentences in the text.

STRATEGY: Encourage students to underline the sentences in the text that correspond to the restatements, and circle those that lead them to make an inference.

ANSWERS

Reading
1. T
2. T
3. F (Almost any emotion — good or bad, happy or sad — can bring on tears.)
4. T
5. T

After you read

A
a. 3   b. 1   c. 6   d. 2   e. 5

Statement b is the main idea of the text.

B
1. not in the text
2. inference (par. 7: Tears are a sign of our ability to feel. If you find yourself near someone crying, deal with it.)
3. restatement (par. 2: "People worry about showing their emotions, afraid that once they lose control, they'll never get it back.")
4. not in the text
5. restatement (par. 1: Still, crying is a fact of life, and your tears are very useful.)
6. not in the text
7. restatement (par. 5: She explains that therapy often consists of giving people permission to cry. She even gives crying exercises, in which patients practice crying just to become used to expressing emotion.)
8. restatement (par. 7: If you find yourself near someone crying, deal with it.)

POSSIBLE ANSWERS

A

1. The students are very bored.
2. He is embarrassed.
3. The child is interested.
4. She is excited.
5. He is tired.
6. He is frustrated.

B

Answers may vary.

Additional activity

Mime, or the art of acting without speech, works very well for demonstrating emotions. Here's a game that uses mime to reinforce vocabulary:

1. Before class, prepare a set of 20 cards with one vocabulary word from the unit written on each.

2. Divide the class into teams of three or four students each. Explain that you will show one person on each team the same word. Then, he or she will use body language and facial expressions to get his or her teammates to guess the word. Remind students that the "actor" may not speak or write any words. The first team to guess the word gets a point. Then, assign another actor for each group. Continue to play as long as there is time and interest.

15 Food

Additional vocabulary

aroma: a strong, usually pleasant smell
bitter: having a strong taste, not salty or sweet
taste buds: cells on the tongue that allow different tastes to be recognized
texture: the way something feels when you touch it
treat: a special and enjoyable food

ANSWERS

What people do with food: chew, slice, smell, swallow
How food tastes: bitter, salty, sour
How people judge food: aroma, flavor, smell, texture

Chocolate

This reading contains some interesting facts about chocolate.

Additional vocabulary

acidity: a sour taste
acne: a disease of the skin in which pimples appear, usually on the face, especially in young people
assess: form a judgment about
dispute: argue against or disagree with
dose: a measured amount of a drug
hint: a small amount of something
hormonal: coming from chemicals in the body that influence the body's growth
lingering: taking longer than usual to leave or disappear
mahogany: reddish brown
myth: a commonly believed but false idea
obesity: the condition of being extremely fat
prejudice: an unfair and unreasonable opinion or feeling

Recognizing point of view

Before students identify the writer's point of view, ask them to look for words and phrases in the text that express someone's opinion. For example, tell them to circle words that refer to the writer's thoughts, preferences, or knowledge.

STRATEGY: Encourage students to circle any words in the text that are related to the points of view listed in the answer choices.

Additional activity

Bring a bar of high quality chocolate and a bar of low quality chocolate to class. Remove the outer wrapper of the chocolate so that students can't see the brand name on the original label. Ask two student volunteers to taste both pieces of chocolate and to guess which one they think is of higher quality and why. Then, show the class the chocolate wrappers, and tell the students whether they were correct. After the students complete the reading and exercises, try the taste test again with two different students. This time, have them use the methods described in the reading to judge the quality of the chocolate.

ANSWERS

Reading

1. F (American surveys show no relationship between chocolate and acne in teenagers.)
2. T
3. F (Chocolate melts in the mouth and is therefore in contact with the teeth for a relatively short time.)
4. F (Chocolate contains only a very small quantity of the substance that causes migraines.)
5. T
6. F (Good quality chocolate contains far less sugar than poor quality chocolate. It's also more expensive, so people are less likely to eat it in large quantities.)

After you read

A

1. c   2. b   3. a

B

3. The writer knows a lot about chocolate.

C

✓: 3, 6
X: 1, 2, 4, 5, 7

What our taste buds say about us

Pages 116-117
This reading presents some research on why people prefer certain foods.

Additional vocabulary

cloudy: not very clear
dish: a particular type of prepared food
hinder: limit the development of something
musical ear: someone who has a *musical ear* is good at music and can hear slight differences in pitch and tone
shape: cause (something) to have a particular character or nature; form
technician: a worker with special skills or knowledge
vacuum-packed: sealed in a container from which most of the air or gas has been removed

Reading skill

Understanding details

See the Teaching suggestions for this skill on page 62.

Additional activity

After students complete the exercises, divide them into groups of three or four. Write the following words on the board: coffee/tea/movies/jazz/pop music/ chocolate/fashion/junk food/restaurants. For each category, tell the groups to discuss which classmate is probably a connoisseur. Then ask the groups to share and explain their answers.

Example: "_____ is probably a connoisseur of movies."

ANSWERS

Reading
All the statements are true.

After you read

A

1. a sweet tooth	4. intensity
2. A sensation	5. tempting
3. A gastronome	6. A connoisseur

B
1. b   2. a   3. a   4. b

It tastes just like chicken

This reading gives travelers advice on how to deal with unfamiliar food.

Additional vocabulary

cast-iron stomach: a stomach able to handle every kind of food
consistency: the degree of thickness of a mixture, especially a liquid
culinary: connected with cooking, especially as a developed skill or art
delicacy: something especially rare or expensive that is good to eat
flatter: use praise to make someone feel important or attractive
glance: look quickly at someone or something
gristly: very hard to chew
paw: the foot of an animal
sizzling: making the sound of frying food
slimy: having a smooth, sticky liquid substance usually considered unpleasant
stew: a dish consisting usually of meat or fish and vegetables cooked slowly in a small amount of liquid
thankfully: pleasantly, but unexpectedly

Additional activity

After students complete the exercises, ask them to look at the use of quotation marks in the reading. Tell them that there are three different reasons that the author of this article has used quotation marks. Working in pairs, have them divide the quoted sentences or phrases according to their use. When pairs find the three uses, ask them to label each group. Then discuss the suggestions as a class.

Direct quotation: "Travel with a cast-iron stomach and eat everything everywhere." (par. 2) "Swallow it quickly." (par. 4) "I still can't tell you what sheep's eyeballs taste like." (par. 4)

A popular expression that people say frequently: "Glad to meet you . . . glad to be doing business with you . . ." (par. 1) "Thanks, but no thanks." (par. 2) "it tastes just like chicken" (par. 4)

To show humor or irony: "it" (par. 4)

ANSWERS

Reading

1, 2, 3, 4

After you read

A

1. people who are going to travel abroad

B

3. American

C

Check items 1, 3, and 4.

1. (Acceptance of the food on your plate means acceptance of host, country, and company.)

3. (Our discomfort comes not so much from the thing itself; it comes from our unfamiliarity with it.)

4. (It helps, though, to slice an item very thin. "Swallow it quickly.")

Cultural note

It tastes just like chicken In the United States, chicken is a very common, popular food. It is something that almost everyone, including children, will eat without objection. To convince someone to try a new food, especially an unfamiliar fish or meat, Americans will often say, "It tastes just like chicken." That means that it is "safe" to eat, and you will not find it disgusting. This expression has become so common that it is often used in a joking, ironic manner, even with food that an American probably *would* find unpleasant.

WRAP-UP

Page 120

POSSIBLE ANSWERS

A

Food flavors: salty, bitter, bland, salty, sour, spicy; *added words*: smoky, chocolaty

Ways of cooking: bake, boil, broil, fry, roast, stir-fry; *added words*: grill, deep-fry

How we eat: chew, bite, swallow; *added words*: suck, lick

Qualities of food: delicious, fattening, healthful; *added words*: oily, greasy

B

1. bite, bland, chew, delicious, healthful, salty, spicy, swallow, taste; *added word*: raw

2. bite, bland, broil, chew, delicious, fattening, fry, salty, swallow, taste; *added word*: juicy

3. bite, chew, delicious, fattening, fry, roast, salty, spicy, stir-fry, swallow, taste; *added word*: crunchy

Additional activity

This game works well for reviewing words that describe food. Write some of the vocabulary from the unit on the board to make the game a little less challenging, for example: bitter, salty, and so on.

1. Before class, prepare a set of 20 cards with a common food item or popular dish written on each.

2. Divide the class into teams of up to ten students each (smaller teams are better).

3. Choose one student from the first team to begin. Show him or her one of the food cards.

4. The student has one minute to describe the food or dish and get his or her team to guess the item. They receive one point if they guess within a set time limit. If not, let another team guess the word to receive a point.

5. Repeat the process until all the teams have had a turn. Continue to play as long as there is time and interest.

16 Sleep & dreams

PREVIEW
Page 121

Additional vocabulary

energize: make (something or someone) more active
function: work effectively
I.Q.: intelligence quotient (a person's level of intelligence measured by standardized tests)
light sleeper: a person who wakes up very easily
nap: sleep for a short time, especially during the day
rejuvenate: make (someone) look or feel energetic again
vivid: producing clear, powerful, and detailed images in the mind

Additional activity

Have students write and conduct a survey about sleep habits and patterns. First, ask them to brainstorm a list of possible questions. Write the questions on the board, and tell them to agree on the five best questions. Using these questions, have students ask their classmates and/or students from other classes about their sleep habits. Then, tell them to summarize the responses for class discussion. Some suggested questions are:

How many hours of sleep do you usually get during the week? On the weekend?
How often do you feel tired?
a) very often   b) occasionally   c) almost never   d) never
Do you think you get enough sleep?
a) Yes   b) No   c) Not sure
How often do you nap?
a) very often   b) occasionally   c) almost never   d) never

Cultural note

Power napping The word *power* before a noun or gerund has a special meaning in American English. It probably comes from the expression *high-powered* — if a person is high-powered, the things they do are important and need lot of energy, skill, experience, knowledge, or responsibility. A *power nap* is a very short period of rest that high-powered people, such as business executives, take to restore their energy so that they can return to work.

Power napping is good for the I.Q.

Pages 122-123

This reading reviews research on sleep and intelligence.

Additional vocabulary

developed world: the countries of the world that have industry and wealth
ill-equipped: not having the ability or equipment to do something well
profound: very strong; extreme
sleep-deprived: not getting the necessary amount of sleep to function
normally

Predicting

Before the students read the text, write the words *power nap* on the board. Ask students to guess the meaning, and write their ideas on the board. After students finish the reading, discuss the guesses again. (If they don't know the words *power* or *nap*, you can define them.)

STRATEGY: To better understand the meaning of compound nouns, encourage students to first think about the meaning of individual parts.

ANSWERS

Reading
1. The amount of sleep people get affects their brain function.

After you read

A

1. d	2. c	3. e	4. a	5. f	6. b

B
1. It affects people's mood, memory, alertness, and performance.
2. They sleep less now. In 1910 the average length of sleep was nine hours, but now it's seven and a half hours.
3. Every hour of sleep lost is equal to a one-point drop in I.Q.
4. Most people need eight hours of sleep, but not all at once. They should sleep for a longer period at night and a shorter period in the afternoon.
5. Workers who take naps are more alert and efficient than those who do not take naps.
6. People need more sleep in winter and less in summer.

This reading answers some frequently asked questions about dreams.

Additional vocabulary

interpretation: an explanation of something's meaning
keep in mind: remember
motive: a reason for doing something
parallel: a similarity between two things
persistent: continuing to do something in a determined way
setting: the place and surroundings where something happens
underlying: real but not immediately obvious
zookeeper: a person who takes care of the animals in a zoo

Reading skill

Understanding details

When students are asked to find answers that are *not* true, encourage them to correct these false statements. This way, you can make sure that they understand the information, and are not simply guessing the answer.

Additional activity

As classwork or homework, assign students a written composition about their dreams. Tell them to use the last two sentences of the text to guide their interpretation. Ask volunteers to read their work aloud. Then collect the compositions.

ANSWERS

Reading
1. Yes, dreams have meaning.
2. Yes, most dreams are in color.
3. Yes, everyone dreams.
4. Think about what each dream element means to you or reminds you of. Then look for parallels between your dreams and your waking life.
5. Something about sleep makes it difficult to remember our dreams. The memory is not lost, but very hard to recall.

After you read

A
1. b   2. c   3. b

B

1. nearly everything that happens throughout the night. Dreams, thoughts that occur, and memories of brief awakening
2. they have difficulty remembering their dreams . . . color is such a natural part of visual experience
3. to debate this issue . . . with their dreams, either by themselves or with others . . . the interpretation very meaningful

READING 3 · What is a dream?

Pages 126-127

This reading presents different theories about dreams.

Additional vocabulary

compensation: something of similar value that you get in place of something   that you need or have lost

dismiss: decide that something or someone is not important and not worth considering

downplay: make something seem less important or not as bad as it really is

fantasy: a pleasant but unlikely situation that you enjoy thinking about

make up for: take the place of (something lost or damaged)

panic: have a strong, sudden feeling of anxiety or fear

show up: appear

wanderings of the mind: thoughts that are not logical or organized

wish-fulfillment: the act of getting something you want

Reading skill

Understanding reference words

To help students understand reference words, cut a paragraph into strips, so that one sentence appears on each strip of paper. Have students work in pairs to put the strips into the correct order. The importance of understanding reference words will become very clear as students complete this exercise.

STRATEGY: Encourage students to look for clues that indicate order. This will allow them to match the reference words to the words or phrases they replace.

ANSWERS

Reading
1, 2, 4, 6, 7, 8

After you read

A
1. a   2. b   3. b   4. b   5. a   6. b

B
1. restatement   5. inference
2. inference   6. restatement
3. not in the text   7. not in the text
4. restatement   8. restatement

WRAP-UP

Page 128

ANSWERS

A
1. e   4. i   7. a
2. d   5. g   8. b
3. c   6. f   9. h

B
1. doze off   5. toss and turn
2. grab some sleep   6. go out like a light
3. drift off   7. sleep in
4. sleep through   8. hit the sack

Additional activity

In pairs, have students choose three or four vocabulary items from the unit to use in a story. Write a model for them to read before they start writing. Encourage them to be creative and to make their stories amusing. Ask volunteers to read their stories aloud, and make note of their vocabulary mistakes. Discuss the errors that day, or collect their stories and make an exercise based on their errors for a later class.

 **Read the text.**

1 When I was young, I wanted to become a singer. Singing always put me in a good mood. It helped me screen out *unpleasant* things, and made me feel that I could tackle any problem. I copied the popular singers that I heard on the radio, *pretending* that I was singing in front of an audience with an orchestra *backing me up*. I sang in a choir and in singing contests. I was certain that my dream would become a reality someday.

2 As a teenager, however, my dream slowly *faded* and was replaced by other interests. Like most of my *peers*, I spent my time worrying about what other people thought about me — especially boys. I still listened to popular music, but I stopped singing. When the leader of the high school choir asked me to join, I refused. I didn't think that "cool" kids sang in the choir. When I grew up, I realized that *giving up* my dream was a mistake.

Complete the exercises.

A Check (✔) the statement that best expresses the main idea of the text. There is only one answer. (*10 points*)

_____ 1. The writer had a very happy childhood because of her love of singing.

_____ 2. The writer feels sorry that she gave up her dream of becoming a singer.

_____ 3. The writer was a very good singer when she was young, but she doesn't sing anymore.

B Check (✔) the statement(s) that are true. There might be more than one answer. (*20 points*)

_____ 1. She won several singing contests when she was young.

_____ 2. She imagined that she was a famous singer when she was young.

_____ 3. She wanted to be like the cool teenagers at her high school.

C Find the words in *italics* in the text. Circle the meaning of each word. (*60 points*)

1. If something is *unpleasant*, it is something **good / bad**.

2. When you *pretend*, you use your **education / imagination**.

3. When someone *backs you up*, they **interrupt / support** you.

4. When a dream *fades*, it becomes **stronger / weaker**.

5. People who are your *peers* are **your / your parents'** age.

6. When you *give up* something, you **continue / stop** doing it.

D The writer could add this sentence to the text. Draw a * in the text where it should be. (*10 points*)

I spent hours choosing the right clothes to impress them.

UNIT 2 QUIZ **Read the text.**

1 Young adults do not usually save money. One possible explanation for this is that they seem to believe that they will be young and able to work forever. Another possible explanation is that people often first become financially independent in their 20s. They are earning money for the first time and it's an *intoxicating* feeling. That first paycheck feels like it is *burning a hole in their pocket*. Many young people are *tempted* to run out and spend it.

2 Also, most young people are no longer living with their families, so their expenses (for example food and rent) are usually as much as or more than the money they make. Even worse, credit cards are easily available, so many young people *incur* huge debts. It can take them years to *get out from under* their credit card debt.

Complete the exercises.

A Check (✔) the correct column. There is only one main idea. (30 points)

		Main idea	Not the main idea	Not in the text
1.	Many young people support themselves for the first time when they are in their 20s.			
2.	Credit cards are difficult to get.			
3.	Most young adults don't save for their future.			

B Find the words in *italics* in the text. Circle the meaning of each word. (50 points)

1. An *intoxicating* feeling is **unpleasant / exciting**.

2. When money *burns a hole in your pocket*, you want to **spend / earn** it.

3. If you are *tempted* to do something, you are **attracted / scared** to do it.

4. When you *incur* a debt, you **pay / owe** money.

5. When you are trying to *get out from under* something, you are trying to **escape from a difficult situation / survive after something falls on top of you**.

C Complete the statements with *more* or *less*. (20 points)

1. Young people usually save _____ money than older people.

2. Some young adults make _____ money than they need to pay their bills.

Name: _____   **Date:** _____

 **Read the text.**

1 For me, teaching is not a job — it is a *vocation*. The word *vocation* comes from the Latin *vocare*, which means "to call." That is how I feel about teaching. I did not look for it — it called me, and I answered.

2 I studied Spanish in college because I wanted to work for an international company. I thought my knowledge of Spanish would *give me an edge* over other possible employees. When I got a job with an international travel company, I was *ecstatic*. Here was a job that *fulfilled* all my needs. However, I soon realized that I was *uncomfortable* working in the business world.

3 Fortunately, my boss gave me a challenge that changed my life. He *put me in charge* of a training program for new employees. When I stood up in front of my first class of trainees, I knew that I had found my calling. A few weeks later, I applied to graduate schools to study to become a teacher.

Complete the exercises.

A Answer the questions. (*40 points*)

1. What does the word *vocation* mean?

2. What kind of job did the writer get when she graduated from college?

3. Was the writer happy when she got her first job?

4. When did the writer realize that being a teacher was the best job for her?

B Find the words in *italics* in the text. Do they have a positive or negative meaning? Mark each positive (+) or negative (−). (*30 points*)

_____ 1. *vocation* (par. 1)   _____ 4. *fulfill* (par. 2)

_____ 2. *give me an edge* (par. 2)   _____ 5. *uncomfortable* (par. 2)

_____ 3. *ecstatic* (par. 2)   _____ 6. *put me in charge* (par. 3)

C Compare the meaning of each pair of sentences. Write same (*S*) or different (*D*). (*30 points*)

_____ 1. I did not look for it.
  I did not find it.

_____ 2. He put me in charge of a training program for new employees.
  He gave me the responsibility of training workers who were new to the company.

_____ 3. Here was a job that fulfilled all my needs.
  I got the job because I had what they needed in an employee.

 **Read the text.**

1 A recent tragic event has focused negative attention on youth sports. During a practice hockey session, the referee and a father of one of the players got into an argument. Their argument quickly became a violent fight. When it ended, the referee was dead from massive head injuries. The strange thing is that the father thought the referee was allowing the game to become too violent!

2 While this case is extreme, it shows a disturbing side of parents in youth sports in North America. If you visit a baseball field on any Saturday morning, you might see parents yelling angrily at both players and umpires. This behavior sends the message to children that winning is everything. It also teaches children that poor sportsmanship and violent behavior are acceptable. We can only hope that the death of the hockey referee will cause adults to take responsibility for making sure that youth sports teach positive values, not violence.

Complete the exercises.

A Which is the best description of the text? Check (✔) the correct answer. (*10 points*)

_____ 1. The text begins with facts. Then it explains the opinions of different groups of people.

_____ 2. The text begins with facts. Then it gives the opinion of the writer.

_____ 3. The text explains the writer's opinion and the opinions of other groups of people.

B Find the words in the text that are related to the words in *italics*. (*60 points*)

1. *tragedy **n.*** (par. 1)   _____ *adj.*

2. *argue **v.*** (par. 1)   _____ *n.*

3. *violence **n.*** (par. 1)   _____ *adj.*

4. *mass **n.*** (par. 1)   _____ *adj.*

5. *disturb **v.*** (par. 2)   _____ *adj.*

6. *behave **v.*** (par. 2)   _____ *n.*

C Check (✔) the three statements that are true. (*30 points*)

_____ 1. The father who killed the referee was afraid that his son might get hurt.

_____ 2. In sports, winning should be more important than anything else.

_____ 3. Many children take part in sports events on the weekends.

_____ 4. Children who take part in sports are more violent than children who are not involved in sports.

_____ 5. Being on a sports team can be a positive experience for children.

 **Read the text.**

1   I have lived my whole life in New England, where the weather is always changing. It is necessary to keep an eye on the weather here. I can't imagine what it is like to live in a place where the weather patterns aren't *changeable* and where memories are not *linked* to a particular season.

2   As a matter of fact, the weather plays an important role in all of my significant memories. The very first memory I have is sitting on top of a high snow bank. I was wearing such a *bulky* snowsuit that it was hard for me to move. I remember staying close to my sister for protection against the *bitter cold* wind. I was only four years old at the time, but four *decades* later, I can still feel the icy cold *seeping* into my bones.

Complete the exercises.

A   Check (✔) the statement that best expresses the main idea of the text. There is only one answer. (*10 points*)

_____ 1. I have lived my whole life in New England, where the weather is always changing.

_____ 2. The weather plays an important role in all of my significant memories.

_____ 3. The very first memory I have is sitting on top of a high snow bank.

B   The writer could add the following sentences to the text. Write each sentence number in the text where it could go. (*30 points*)

1. Her body was my only shelter.

2. I know that I'll always remember that winter day.

3. If you don't, you might be surprised when you leave your house in the morning.

C   Find the words in *italics* in the text. Then complete the sentences. (*60 points*)

changeable (par. 1)   *bulky* (par. 2)   *decade* (par. 2)

linked (par. 1)   *bitter cold* (par. 2) *seeping* (par. 2)

1. When two things are _____ , they are closely connected to each other.

2. _____ weather is exciting and unpredictable.

3. On a _____ day, you should wear a heavy coat.

4. A _____ is a time period of ten years.

5. Wearing _____ clothes can make you feel big, clumsy, and awkward.

6. If cold air is _____ into your house, it comes in slowly through a crack or small opening.

 **Read the text.**

1 Recently, some people have suggested that a stricter atmosphere is needed in the public schools. One of the *proposed regulations* requires all students to wear uniforms. This is a clear violation of students' rights, and it will not work.

2 People in favor of school uniforms claim that they tear down social barriers. They believe that these barriers are created when some students, who are able to buy expensive outfits, make fun of classmates who can't afford them. People who favor school uniforms also argue that allowing students to wear their own clothes leads to a daily fashion competition that takes students' attention away from learning.

3 These might seem like *convincing arguments*. However, anyone who attended a school where students have to wear uniforms knows better. Teenagers are especially eager to follow fashion trends. If we force students to wear uniforms, they will find another way to express their fashion sense, such as buying stylish book bags or wearing the latest hairstyles. Unfortunately, it's not that easy to eliminate social differences.

Complete the exercises.

A Mark each sentence true (*T*), false (*F*), or does not give the information (*?*). (*40 points*)

_____ 1. Many private schools already require school uniforms.

_____ 2. Classmates may laugh at students who can't afford stylish clothing.

_____ 3. Teenagers are less interested in fashion than younger children.

_____ 4. Requiring uniforms is just one of the proposed changes to public schools.

B Mark each argument for (*F*) or against (*A*) school uniforms. (*40 points*)

_____ 1. Some students make fun of classmates.

_____ 2. Students will find another way to express their fashion sense.

_____ 3. It's not that easy to eliminate social barriers.

_____ 4. Some students can buy expensive outfits.

C Circle the correct answers. (*20 points*)

1. When you *propose* something, you make a suggestion. When you *regulate* something, you control it by making a rule. *Proposed regulations* (par. 1) are
   a. rules that have been suggested.   b. suggestions that are legal.

2. When you *convince* someone of something, you cause him or her to believe you. A *convincing argument* (par. 3) is
   a. a true argument.   b. a strong argument.

 **Read the text.**

1 Meeting a person from another country can sometimes cause confusion. The most interesting example of cross-cultural misunderstanding that I experienced involved a student from Kuwait. I was a *novice* English educator, and Ahmed was my first Middle Eastern student.

2 When Ahmed stared at me blankly one day, I asked him if he understood the lesson. He *drew* his eyebrows together, moved his chin upward, and made a 'tsk' sound by *tapping* his tongue against the roof of his mouth. To an American, this gesture means "Yes, of course. What a question!" so I continued with my presentation. *Immediately*, Ahmed began waving his hands in the air, saying, "No understand!" Now it was my turn to look lost. Ahmed was having trouble *keeping up*. Years later, I discovered that in Kuwait and many other parts of the Middle East, an upward *motion* of the chin expresses "No!"

3 Early experiences like this gave me a deep appreciation for the importance of body language in intercultural encounters.

Complete the exercises.

A Who do you think the text was written for? Check (✔) the correct answer. (10 points)

_____ 1. Kuwaiti parents who want to send their children to study abroad

_____ 2. teachers of English language courses

_____ 3. specialists in body language and communication

B Find the words in *italics* in the text. Then match each word with its meaning. (60 points)

_____ 1. *novice* (par.1)   a. stay level or equal with the other students

_____ 2. *draw* (par. 2)   b. inexperienced

_____ 3. *tap* (par. 2)   c. movement

_____ 4. *immediately* (par. 2)   d. touch lightly and quickly

_____ 5. *keep up* (par. 2)   e. pull

_____ 6. *motion* (par. 2)   f. without delay

C Check (✔) the statements that describe Ahmed. (30 points)

_____ 1. He often felt confused and uncomfortable in class.

_____ 2. He was unfriendly to his teacher.

_____ 3. His understanding of English was incomplete.

_____ 4. He was unsuccessful in communicating with his teacher.

_____ 5. His body language was unacceptable in the Middle East.

Read the text.

1 In 1962, a forty-one-year-old astronaut named John Glenn became the first American to orbit the earth in a spacecraft. The *accomplishments* of Glenn and his colleagues in the NASA Space Program inspired the popular novel and Academy Award-winning film *The Right Stuff*.

2 But John Glenn's story does not end with his achievements in space. In 1974, John Glenn was elected as a United States senator, an important political position in the United States government. He served as a senator for 22 years. In 1984, he ran for the U.S. presidency. However, his *campaign* for president was *ultimately* unsuccessful.

3 In 1998, John Glenn returned to space again, this time becoming the oldest astronaut ever to orbit the earth. When he was asked why he wanted to return to space at the age of 77, Glenn *replied*, "I wanted to go back up as soon as I got down. You're on the *cutting edge* of science. That's fascinating to me. I always thought if ever there was an opportunity, I would do it [again]."

Complete the exercises.

A Find the words in *italics* in the text. Then match each word with its meaning. (*50 points*)

_____ 1. *accomplishment* (par. 1)   a. an attempt to get elected to a political office

_____ 2. *campaign* (par. 2)   b. a very new, modern development

_____ 3. *ultimately* (par. 2)   c. an achievement

_____ 4. *reply* (par. 3)   d. in the end; finally

_____ 5. *cutting edge* (par. 3)   e. answer

B Number the sentences from 1 (first event) to 5 (last event). (*30 points*)

_____ a. John Glenn tried to become president of the United States.

_____ b. John Glenn became the oldest astronaut to go up in space.

_____ c. John Glenn became the first American to orbit the earth.

_____ d. John Glenn became a U.S. senator.

_____ e. John Glenn retired from the U.S. Senate.

C Answer the questions. (*20 points*)

1. In what year did John Glenn retire from the U.S. Senate?

_____

2. What are three things that John Glenn is famous for?

_____

Read the text.

1 Taking care of a pet can teach children some *valuable* lessons. One lesson pets can teach children is that their actions have real *consequences*. If a child forgets to feed a pet, it will get sick, suffer, and might even die. Another lesson pets can teach is *compassion*. Children can be selfish, but taking care of a pet forces them to consider the needs of another living creature. Finally, pets can teach children valuable lessons about life and death. Dealing with the death of a beloved pet can help children understand that life is beautiful yet *fragile*.

2 The type of pet that parents choose for their children should be based on the amount of responsibility the child is ready for. Fish, for example, need only food and a clean environment to live. On the other hand, dogs have emotional and physical needs, and require exercise, love, and *companionship*. Whether the pet is a cat, dog, fish, or bird, the important thing is that the child is responsible for its care.

Complete the exercises.

A Check (✔) the statement that best expresses the main idea of the text. (*10 points*)

_____ 1. Children can be selfish, but taking care of a pet forces them to consider the needs of another living creature.

_____ 2. Dealing with the death of a beloved pet can help children understand that life is beautiful yet fragile.

_____ 3. Taking care of a pet can teach children some valuable lessons.

B Find the words in *italics* in the text. Circle the meaning of each word. (*50 points*)

1. If something is *valuable*, it is **easy to do** / **important**.

2. *Consequences* are **results of an action** / **causes of a problem**.

3. If you have *compassion*, you feel **sympathy and sadness** / **envy and dislike** for others.

4. If something is *fragile*, it is **very strong/ not very strong**.

5. If you enjoy *companionship*, you like being **with someone** / **independent**.

C Check (✔) the correct column. (*40 points*)

		General statement	Specific example
1.	Another lesson pets can teach is compassion.		
2.	Pets can teach children that their actions have real consequences.		
3.	If a child forgets to feed a pet, it will get sick, suffer, and might even die.		
4.	Taking care of a pet forces children to consider the needs of another living creature.		

Name: _____   **Date:** _____

 **Read the text.**

1 Traveling can be a wonderful adventure. Traveling by airplane, however, can be very tiring. Follow these *tips* to *minimize* the *discomfort* of your next long plane trip.

2 Don't pack too much. It's not fun carrying a heavy suitcase around everywhere. Instead, pack only what you know you are going to wear. Choose clothes that can be worn together. For example, take one pair of pants and three matching tops.

3 In your carry-on bag (a small bag that you keep with you on the plane), pack your toothbrush, medications, and any other important personal items. Also, pack some extra clothes so that you can survive if your suitcase is lost.

4 Try to book a seat on the earliest flight of the day. Delays are less likely if your flight is the first one to depart.

5 Drink plenty of water during the flight. People often become *dehydrated* when they fly. This makes them feel tired and ill. Drinking a lot of water will make you feel more *refreshed* when you arrive at your destination.

Complete the exercises.

A Find the words in *italics* in the text. Circle the correct answers. (*50 points*)

1. A *tip* is _____ .
   a. money　　　　　　b. advice　　　　　　　　　c. the top

2. If you *minimize* something, you _____ .
   a. make it stronger　　b. make it more interesting　　c. make it smaller

3. When you feel *discomfort*, you are _____ .
   a. happy　　　　　　b. upset　　　　　　　　　c. uneasy

4. Someone who is *dehydrated* needs _____ .
   a. cool air　　　　　b. water　　　　　　　　　c. rest

5. If you are *refreshed*, you feel _____ .
   a. much better　　　b. very excited　　　　　　c. a little sick

B Mark each statement restatement (*R*) or inference (*I*). (*40 points*)

_____ 1. A black pair of pants is a good thing to pack when you travel.

_____ 2. The first flight of the day is more likely to leave on time than the last flight of the day.

_____ 3. Your body will suffer if you don't drink enough water during the flight.

_____ 4. It's a good idea to pack a comb or hairbrush in your carry-on bag.

C Write your own tip to add to the list. (*10 points*)

_____

_____

Name: _____   Date: _____

 **Read the text.**

1 My grandmother is 94 years old, so you can imagine the number of world-shaking inventions she has seen during her life — automobiles, televisions, airplane travel, space exploration, answering machines, VCRs, personal computers, cell phones — and the list goes on. She *gracefully* accepted most of these advances in technology. With the Internet, however, she finally *met her match*. Although she is not old-fashioned and is more active than many people her age, she has decided that she is too old to *master* the Internet.

2 As a big *fan* of the Internet, I am trying to change her attitude. After all, she knows how to program a VCR, which I think is more difficult than logging on to the Internet! But she insists that at her age, she will let the latest "marvel of the age" *pass her by*. Who can argue with that?

Complete the exercises.

A Check (✔) the statements that are true. (*40 points*)

_____ 1. The writer's grandmother does not like new things.

_____ 2. The writer and her grandmother do not get along with each other.

_____ 3. The writer's grandmother owns a VCR.

_____ 4. The writer's grandmother has probably traveled in an airplane.

B Find the words in *italics* in the text. Then complete the sentences. (*50 points*)

gracefully (par. 1)   *master* (par. 1)   *pass her by* (par. 2)

met her match (par. 1)   *fan* (par. 2)

1. He accepts difficulties _____ . He never complains about anything.

2. I am a soccer _____ . I never miss an important game.

3. My friend is always trying new things. She says that she doesn't want life to _____ .

4. She is a great chess player, but yesterday she _____ . It was the first time she lost a game.

5. If you _____ an activity, you become skilled at it.

C What is the writer's attitude toward her grandmother? Check (✔) the correct answer. (*10 points*)

_____ 1. worried   _____ 3. loving

_____ 2. confused   _____ 4. angry

UNIT 12 QUIZ Read the text.

1 Do you believe animals *form* friendships with other animals? In the case of dogs, the answer is definitely "Yes!" To prove my point, try this simple *experiment*.

2 Go to a park or another area where people take their dogs. Choose one dog to observe. You will notice that the dog *reacts* differently to different dogs. While he pays absolutely no attention to some dogs, he treats others with obvious dislike. However, when that one "special" dog arrives, he gets very excited. The two friends run around in circles, obviously *delighted* to be together. Like a loyal, trustworthy friend, he is always there when one of his *canine* friends gets into a fight and needs his support. If you watch for several days, you will see that the dog is consistent in the way he treats other dogs.

3 It is well known that man's best friend is a dog, but you might be surprised to discover that a dog's best friend is almost certainly another dog!

Complete the exercises.

A Check (✔) the statement that best expresses the main idea of the text. There is only one answer. (10 points)

_____ 1. A dog reacts differently to different dogs.

_____ 2. Animals form friendships with other animals.

_____ 3. A dog's best friend is almost certainly another dog.

B Circle the correct answer. (40 points)

1. When dogs greet each other, they

   a. always get excited.   b. get excited if they like each other.

2. When a dog's "friend" gets into a fight,

   a. the dog will run away.   b. the dog will always help him.

3. A dog's behavior toward a "friend" is

   a. very dependable.   b. very changeable.

4. Many people say that

   a. man's best friend is a dog.   b. dogs like dogs more than people.

C Find the words in *italics* in the text. Circle the meaning of each word. (50 points)

1. *form* (par. 1)   a. make   b. end

2. *experiment* (par. 1)   a. proof   b. a test

3. *react* (par. 2)   a. behave   b. jump up

4. *delighted* (par. 2)   a. respectful   b. very happy

5. *canine* (par. 2)   a. human   b. dog

 **Read the text.**

1 Gift giving traditions vary from country to country. Knowing some basic customs can save you a lot of embarrassment when you travel. Here are some rules for gift giving in the United States.

2 If you are invited to someone's home for dinner, you should bring a small gift to show your appreciation to the host or hostess. A bouquet of flowers or a box of chocolates is an appropriate gift for this occasion.

3 If you are invited to a wedding, find out the name of the store where the couple is registered. When you go there, give the sales clerk the couple's name, and you will get a list of possible gifts. You can be sure the couple will like whatever you buy. After all, they wrote the list themselves!

4 Finally, only elementary school students give presents to their teachers — and it is the student's choice, not an obligation. It is not expected and not considered appropriate for university students to give gifts to their professors.

Complete the exercises.

A What do these words refer to? (50 points)

1. *this occasion* (par. 2, line 3)   _____

2. *there* (par. 3, line 2)   _____

3. *they* (par. 3, line 4)   _____

4. *their* (par. 4, line 1)   _____

5. *it* (par. 4, line 2)   _____

B Who do you think the text was written for? Check (✔) the correct answer. (10 points)

_____ 1. school children in the United States

_____ 2. foreign students coming to study in the United States

_____ 3. tourists planning a vacation to the United States

C Find the words in the text that are related to the words in *italics*. (40 points)

1. *variation **n.*** (par. 1)   _____ *v.*

2. *registration **n.*** (par. 3)   _____ *v.*

3. *choose **v.*** (par. 4)   _____ *n.*

4. *obligated **adj.*** (par. 4)   _____ *n.*

 **Read the text.**

1 Children who suffer from a *disorder* called autism find it difficult or even impossible to show emotions in a normal way. Parents and the people who take care of autistic children often describe them as being emotionless. They don't *make eye contact*, and they don't seem to notice other people. They often perform *repetitive behaviors*, such as rocking back and forth, or repeat meaningless phrases. Sometimes, autistic children stop talking completely.

2 These behaviors can be frustrating for the parents of an autistic child, who often feel powerless and *guilty*. Many parents think that they are responsible for their child's condition. In fact, doctors believe that the disorder may have a physical cause, related to a problem in the development of the brain. It is not clear why, but some children *grow out of* their autism as they mature, and go on to lead normal lives.

Complete the exercises.

A Find the words in *italics* in the text. Circle the meaning of each word. (*50 points*)

1. A person who suffers from a *disorder* has **physical or mental problems / strong emotions**.

2. When you *make eye contact* with someone, you **look at / meet** the person.

3. A *repetitive behavior* is an action that you **enjoy doing / repeat**.

4. You feel **very embarrassed / you have done something wrong** when you feel *guilty*.

5. If you *grow out of* something, you **don't do it anymore / stop growing**.

B Answer the questions. Write (?) if the text does not give the information. (*50 points*)

1. How do parents feel about the behavior of their autistic children?

   _____

2. What is the most likely cause of autism?

   _____

3. What are some of the signs that a child is autistic?

   _____

4. At what age do children usually become autistic?

   _____

5. Why do some autistic children go on to lead normal lives?

   _____

 **Read the text.**

1 Have you ever *wondered* when humans first started to cook? Until recently, most scientists believed that our ancestors began using fire to cook food about 500,000 years ago. However, Harvard University professor Dr. Richard Wrangham thinks humans discovered cooking much earlier — about 1.5 million years earlier.

2 Dr. Wrangham bases his *theory* on several things. First, he points to the small jaw and rounded teeth of humans of 1.9 million years ago. He believes that early humans' jaws got smaller and their teeth became rounder because they started cooking their food. This made it softer and easier to eat. Second, when he studied 48 types of plant foods that early humans ate, he found that the body can't *digest* 21 of them unless they are cooked. Finally, he points to the fact that 2 million years ago, the size of the human brain and body increased. He believes that our ancestors were getting bigger because they were eating a more healthful diet of cooked foods.

Complete the exercises.

A Check (✔) the statement that best expresses the main idea of the text. There is only one answer. (10 points)

_____ 1. When human beings started to use fire to cook their food 2 million years ago, they got bigger and stronger.

_____ 2. A Harvard University professor thinks that early humans started cooking their food 1.5 million years earlier than previously believed.

_____ 3. Cooking food makes it easier for the body to digest, and easier to chew.

B Find the words in *italics* in the text. Circle the meaning of each word. (30 points)

1. When you *wonder* about something, you **answer / think about** it.

2. If you have a *theory*, you **suggest a possible explanation / state the facts**.

3. If your body can't *digest* something, it can't **use it for energy / taste it**.

C Answer the questions. (30 points)

1. When did human beings first start to cook their food?

_____

2. What is the relationship between cooking and smaller jaws and rounder teeth?

_____

3. What caused the human brain and body to increase in size 2 million years ago?

_____

D What do these words refer to? Circle the correct answer. (30 points)

1. *This* (par. 2, line 4)   a. cooking their food   b. smaller jaws and rounder teeth

2. *it* (par. 2, line 4)   a. their food   b. eating

3. *they* (par. 2, line 6)   a. 48 types of plants   b. 21 types of plants

 **Read the text.**

1   For many years, I had the same vivid dream over and over again, sometimes several times nightly. In my dream, I was always driving a car in which the front seat was so far from the *brakes* that I couldn't reach them. As the car began to go faster and faster, I would wake up in a *panic*. For years I tried unsuccessfully to understand the significance of this.

2   Then one day as I was driving home from work, I had a sudden memory of myself. I was five years old and behind the *wheel* of a moving car. The minute I got home, I called my mother and asked her about it. She answered, "Don't you remember? When you were five years old, you were playing in your father's car, which was parked at the top of a hill. Somehow, you put the car into gear, and it started rolling down the hill and hit a tree. The car was damaged, but you were fine — just a little frightened."

3   Can you believe that I have never had that dream again?

Complete the exercises.

A What do these words refer to? (*40 points*)

1. *them* (par. 1, line 3)   _____

2. *this* (par. 1, line 5)   _____

3. *which* (par. 2, line 5)   _____

4. *it* (par. 2, line 5)   _____

B Check (✔) the statements that are true. (*30 points*)

_____ 1. In the writer's dream, the car always crashed into a tree.

_____ 2. The writer really wanted to understand the meaning of his dream.

_____ 3. The writer never had the dream again because he finally knew what caused it.

_____ 4. The writer couldn't stop the car because his legs were too short.

C Find the words in *italics* in the text. Circle the meaning of each word. (*30 points*)

1. If your *brakes* fail, you cannot **start / stop** your car.

2. If you are in a state of *panic*, you are feeling very **nervous / patient**.

3. The *wheel* is used to **stop / turn** the car.

Unit quiz answers

UNIT 1 QUIZ

A

2

B

2, 3

C

1. bad
2. imagination
3. support
4. weaker
5. your
6. stop

D

par. 2, after: I spent my time worrying about what other people thought about me — especially boys.

UNIT 2 QUIZ

A

1. not the main idea
2. not in the text
3. main idea

B

1. exciting
2. spend
3. attracted
4. owe
5. escape from a difficult situation

C

1. less
2. less

UNIT 3 QUIZ

A

1. The word *vocation* comes from the Latin *vocare*, meaning "to call."
2. The writer got a job with an international travel company.
3. The writer was "ecstatic" when she got her first job because it fulfilled all her needs.
4. The writer realized that being a teacher was the best job for her when stood up in front of her first class of trainees.

B

1. +   2. +   3. +   4. +   5. -   6. +

C

1. D
2. S
3. D

UNIT 4 QUIZ

A

2

B

1. tragic
2. argument
3. violent
4. massive
5. disturbing
6. behavior

C

1, 3, 5

UNIT 5 QUIZ

A

2

B

1. par. 2, after: . . . close to my sister for protection against the bitter cold wind.
2. par. 2, after: . . . I can still feel the icy cold seeping into my bones.
3. par. 1, after: . . . It is necessary to keep an eye on the weather here.

C

1. linked
2. Changeable
3. bitter cold
4. decade
5. bulky
6. seeping

UNIT 6 QUIZ

A

1. ?
2. T
3. F (Teenagers are *especially* eager to follow fashion trends.)
4. T

B

1. F   2. A   3. A   4. F

C
1. a
2. b

UNIT 7 QUIZ

A
2

B
1. b   2. e   3. d   4. f   5. a   6. c

C
1, 3, 4

UNIT 8 QUIZ

A
1. c   2. a   3. d   4. e   5. b

B
a. 3   b. 5   c. 1   d. 2   e. 4

C
1. John Glenn retired from the U.S. Senate in 1996.
2. John Glenn was the first American to orbit the earth. He was a U.S. senator for 22 years. He ran for the U.S presidency. He is the oldest astronaut ever to orbit the earth. His accomplishments inspired *The Right Stuff*. (**Note:** Only three answers are necessary for full credit.)

UNIT 9 QUIZ

A
3

B
1. important
2. results of an action
3. sympathy and sadness
4. not very strong
5. with someone

C
1. general statement
2. general statement
3. specific example
4. specific example

UNIT 10 QUIZ

A
1. b   2. c   3. c   4. b   5. a

B
1. I   2. R   3. R   4. I

C
Answers will vary.

UNIT 11 QUIZ

A
3, 4

B
1. gracefully
2. fan
3. pass her by
4. met her match
5. master

C
3

UNIT 12 QUIZ

A
3

B
1. b   2. b   3. a   4. a

C
1. a   2. b   3. a   4. b   5. b

UNIT 13 QUIZ

A
1. an invitation to someone's home for dinner
2. the store where the couple is registered
3. the couple
4. elementary school students'
5. giving a gift/whether to give the teacher a present

B
2

C
1. vary
2. registered
3. choice
4. obligation

UNIT 14 QUIZ

A
1. physical or mental problems
2. look at
3. repeat
4. you have done something wrong
5. don't do it anymore

B
1. Parents feel frustrated, powerless, and guilty about the behavior of their autistic children.
2. The most likely cause of autism is a problem in the development in the brain.
3. Autistic children may seem emotionless, don't make eye contact, don't seem to notice other people, often engage in repetitive behaviors, repeat meaningless phrases, or stop talking completely.
4. ?
5. ?

UNIT 15 QUIZ

A
2

B
1. think about
2. suggest a possible explanation
3. use it for energy

C
1. Until recently, scientists believed human beings began cooking food about 500,000 years ago. Dr. Wrangham, however, believes that humans started cooking about 1.5 million years earlier (or about 2 million years ago).
2. When early humans began cooking their food, it was softer and easier to eat, so they didn't need such big jaws or sharp teeth.
3. The size of the human brain and body increased because they were eating a more healthful diet of cooked foods.

D
1. a
2. a
3. b

UNIT 16 QUIZ

A
1. the brakes
2. the dream
3. father's car/the car
4. father's car/the car

B
2, 3, 4

C
1. stop
2. nervous
3. turn